**Always
be
natural**

To Meryl
 With every
best to you and
your dear husband
— and God Bless you
as a Deacon in
Emmanuel Love
 Gethin

Always be natural

by
Gethin Hughes MBE.

First published in Great Britain in 2006 by
Bryngold Books Ltd.,
Golden Oaks, 98 Brynau Wood, Cimla,
Neath, South Wales, SA11 3YQ.
www.bryngoldbooks.com

Typesetting, layout and design
by Bryngold Books

Copyright © Gethin Hughes 2006

All rights reserved. No part of this publication may be reproduced, stored in a retrieval system, or transmitted in any form, or by any means, electronic, mechanical, photocopying, recording, or otherwise without the prior permission, in writing, of the copyright holder, nor be otherwise circulated in any form or binding or cover other than that in which it is published and without a similar condition being imposed on the subsequent publisher.

ISBN 0-9547859-6-7

Printed in Wales by
Dinefwr Press, Rawlings Road,
Llandybie, Carmarthenshire, SA18 3YD

Contents

Foreword	7
Going Solo	11
In Concert	15
Flash Harry	23
Initial Impression	25
Electric Example	29
Spirit Raiser	31
Wake-up Call	33
Twin Talents	37
Rainbow Man	39
Lively Lessons	43
Perfect Harmony	47
Street Star	51
Preaching Power	53
Three of a Kind	55
Signature Sounds	59
Civic Salute	61
Stitches and Stamps	65
Knight of Knights	67
Welcome Visits	69
Triniti Team	71
Winging It	73
String Time	75
Fairy Godmother	77
Royal Appointment	81
Bread of Heaven	83
Tucking In	85
With Heart and Voice	86
Music Masters	91
Platform Personality	93
Playing the Game	95
Ivory Queen	99
Family of Fame	103
Clean Easy	107
Sweet Songsters	111
Don't Kill Mother	115
Musical Magic	119
Delightful Discovery	121
Saving the Day	125
Wifely Wonder	127
Clever Cousins	129
All That Jazz	133
Hit For Six	135
Dockland Duo	137
Dramatic Entry	139
Trademark Tune	143
Father's Footsteps	147
Nightingale Notes	149
Shining Lights	151
First Lady	153
Rule Britannia	155
Rocks of Ages	157
Curtain Raisers	163
Cruise Companion	165
Larger Than Life	169
Heavenly Harpist	173
Shopping Spree	177
Caring Community	183

Appreciation

Many people have played a part in making this publication possible.
Particular appreciation is afforded to:
Llanelli Town Council, Carmarthenshire County Council,
Llanelli Historical Society,
Mark Jewell, Llanelli Borough librarian; Alun Ebenezer,
Peter Alban Morris, Olwen Whomsley, Dilys Williams,
Betty Herbert, Noela Williams, Margaret Skinner,
Carol Morgan, David Ffrancon Lloyd-Davies,
Annette Gravell, Eirwen Taylor, Gowerton; John Edwards,
John Bowen, Sandy Road; Alan John, Pontarddulais;
Margaret Williams, Nancy and Moelwyn Williams, Gowerton;
Doreen Thomas, West Cross, Swansea; Peter Thomas, Graham James,
Violet McIntyre, Ellesmere; Rev. & Mrs Emrys Thomas, Caernarfon;
Staff of the Llanelli Star, Spencer Feeney, Robert Lloyd,
David and Cheryl Roberts of Bryngold Books.

Dedication

*This book is dedicated to Patricia — my friend and cousin,
and the congregation of Triniti Chapel, Llanelli.*

Foreword

Taking on the editorship of a popular weekly newspaper, you would expect to inherit many things from your predecessor. A solid desk, a trusty typewriter (yes, it was that long ago) and a reliable contacts book, perhaps? But the Llanelli Star, back in 1989, also came with a columnist, our 'Geth', Gethin Hughes MBE, Llanelli's very own Mr Music and a man with enough 'been there, seen it, met them and done it' stories to fill a book.

What started off as a weekly newspaper project – Solo Note with Gethin Hughes – has now taken on new life as a book and, who knows, this could just be the first volume of Geth's tales? It was, of course, always Geth's intention that his words would one day appear in book form. We spent countless hours discussing the project and no-one is more delighted than I am to see his wish come true.

It all started way back in 1986 when my predecessor, Spencer Feeney, took over as Editor of the Llanelli Star after the death of Geoffrey D Lloyd.
Geoffrey – a gifted musician – was a vice-president of the Llanelli Young Music Lovers' Association, a group very dear to Gethin's heart. The tales Gethin wove during rehearsals for Spencer's wedding to his wife Jacqui at Waunarlwydd – Gethin was the organist – provided the spark for what was to be one of the longest-running newspaper columns in the history of journalism in Wales.

Gethin's Solo Notes has long since finished its run in the Star, but it is a testament to the column's popularity that we are frequently asked if there are plans to re-run the stories. This book will, hopefully, fill that need – being a rich seam of anecdotes from all four corners of the globe. It is liberally sprinkled with stardust and hopefully reflects Gethin's admirable 'game for anything' qualities. From scuba diving off The Great Barrier Reef to riding a mechanical bucking bronco at a Wild West centre in Denver to playing out his inimitable party pieces at post-concert Cor Meibion concerts, nothing is too much of a challenge for Gethin.

It would take another book to recount anecdotes from life on the road with Gethin. But two memories in particular will have to suffice our purposes here – First, there was the occasion when Cor Meibion Llanelli, on their 2001 tour of North America, stopped off at the Golden Gate bridge in San Francisco for a sight-seeing tour. As usual, Gethin was the proud owner of the loudest shirt of the day, a tropical fruit-splashed kaleidoscope which would put anything Hawaiian in the shade. With our musical director confined to base camp for eisteddfod judging, Gethin proceeded to climb on top of a park bench and lead the choir in a quick 10-minute medley of items "Gee, who

Gethin Hughes with his MBE and, inset, the proud moment when he received the award from Her Majesty The Queen.

is that guy?" one passing American tourist was heard to ask. "That's our Gethin, he's played for Gracie Fields," a helpful chorister responded.
"No kidding . . . what position?" asked the puzzled American who misheard and was frantically trying to work out which American Football team played at Gracie Fields! Second, there was the celebrated last night on tour when Gethin kept the troops entertained while we attempted to re-book 110 travelling choristers on flights out of Minneapolis to Chicago following several post 9/11 'no fly' days Stateside.

It was a complicated evening, made much more humorous by Gethin's rendition of The Biggest Aspidistra in the World! And, of course, predictably, I was called upon to act as his foil as 'Walter' during his closing party piece. Fortunately, Gethin remains such a friend that I can forgive him — even after suffering that humiliation!

He remains a Llanelli treasure.

**Robert Lloyd
Editor,
Llanelli Star**
April 2006

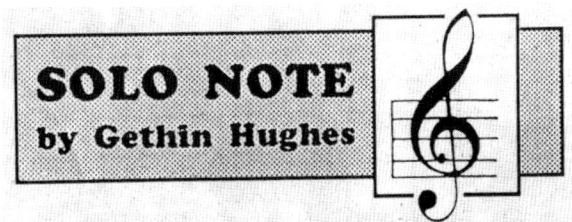

The familiar Llanelli Star newspaper heading that identified the decade-long column which gave birth to this book.

This picture is where it all began. It shows me as a tiny babe in arms with three older generations of my family. They are my mother, who is nursing me, my grandmother and great grandmother.

Going Solo
The journey begins

Our busy lives rarely afford us sufficient time to stand still and ponder on what has gone before, but when the opportunity to cast an over-the-shoulder glance does arrive, the memories it rekindles can often surprise. One moment it seems that we are preparing to embark on an exciting journey through life and the next we are left wondering where the years — now heavily punctuated by people, places, experiences and events — have gone. Such thoughts have rarely been absent since I began to focus on some of my own particular milestones, something with which many will surely empathise.

The excuse to do so was inspired by that laudable organ of local record the Llanelli Star — or at least one of its former editors, Spencer Feeney. He had been listening intently as I shared some anecdotes born of my lifelong association with the town and a love of music and its making, when he suggested I put pen to paper and share some of them in a regular column for the paper. At first I resisted, unsure of what I could write about. "The people you have met and your friends in Llanelli," replied Spencer confidently. His gentle persuasiveness eventually conquered my shyness to swap some of my time with the black and white of a musical keyboard for the identical colours of a newspaper column. Early nervousness about the reaction to my literary rather than musical compositions soon diminished. Readers, I was assured, enjoyed it and continued to do so for the near-decade that it continued, recalling many of the musical greats I had met in my life both local and international — in Llanelli and out of town.

When I sat down, apprehensively, to write the very first Gethin's Solo Notes — as the column became known — I made one important decision. I promised myself that I would always endeavour to be natural, just as I had in life. It seemed to work. There was an amazing response to each fresh topic as the columns grew in number, encouraged further by Spencer Feeney's successor as editor, Robert Lloyd. When the sad day dawned for my final 'notes' both helped nurture the idea of a compilation in book form.

In a way I have been fortunate to have accomplished many things in my lifetime so far and it is amazing when one adds up all the years spent immersed in one way or another in the world of music. To me it has been a delight. To the fresh eye it might seem like a scoreboard — I have been organist at Triniti Presbyterian Chapel for 37 years, performed in my voluntary variety concert party for 50 years, given around 1,400 concerts for hospitals, homes, church and chapel societies, WIs and youth clubs, accompanied a host of well-known soloists, been organist for the Royal National Eisteddfod of Wales, given organ recitals and concerts in prestigious venues at home

Family life is something that has always been important to me, seen here as a young teenager on holiday in North Wales with Mam and Dad.

and abroad including including St David's Cathedral, the Royal Albert Hall; Mormon Tabernacle, Salt Lake City, USA and Nidaros Cathedral in Trondheim, Norway. I have entertained, albeit unofficially, on ocean-going cruise liners and even played for many of the 57 National Eisteddfod Blue Riband winners the past 60 years have given us including: Megan Holiday, the very first winner in 1943, and for nearly a decade I have been accompanist to Cor Meibion Llanelli. I was also the founder of the Llanelli Young Music Lovers' Association which ran for more than 25 years. It has been a tuneful time that was enjoyable combined with a rewarding career in teaching. In addition to this I was delighted, as a tribute to my 50 years as an accompanist, to have an LP record produced by Sain Records on which I played alongside singers Arthur Davies and Aled Edwards and honoured to be awarded an MBE for services to music in Wales in the New Year's Honours list of 1998, receiving the award on March 4, that year, from Her Majesty the Queen.

Gathering together the material for this book brought it all flooding back — the different characters, variety of events, people's dress in chapel concerts, along with stories shared many years before. There were countless musical excursions too, meetings with stars of stage, screen, radio and TV, plus a lingering fondness for the friendships forged at work, rest and play, not least during the 50 year lifespan of my popular concert party. Not bad for a former Strade school music teacher who overcame the handicap of failing his 11-plus examination. Central to it all has been Llanelli. A great Welsh town with wonderful people, their community spirit second to none and of course my great love, from an early age of music, a passport to many of my travels and adventures. That perhaps is where Mam must put in an appearance. For although both my mother and father were at all times supportive, it was my mother's influence that set me on the road to the musicianship I proudly claim for my own today and have always enjoyed sharing.

My mother and father were married in Triniti Chapel, Llanelli in June 1932 before making their home with my grandparents in Hick Street, where on July 3, 1935 at precisely 11.15pm I was born in the back bedroom of Deganwy, the name the house proudly bears to this day. Mam nurtured me in the Welsh culture and I loved it. She taught me verses and psalms along with short poems which I would recite in Triniti chapel. That was just the precursor to the time in 1943 when she began taking me to concerts, dramas, plays and pantomimes to see and hear a whole host of leading performers. I loved these unforgettable musical treats, in both Welsh and English.

Mam also took me to chapel concerts and eisteddfodau, then the Glenalla operettas and those at Morfa Primary School. When Llanelli's Market Hall was renovated and reopened as the New Public Hall, she also took me to many performances there as well as arranging special trips to the Swansea Empire for pantomimes, variety shows and musicals. On the formation of the Welsh National Opera Company in 1946, I was taken twice a year to performances that included La Traviata, Carmen, Il Trovatore, La Boheme and Nabucco.

When I was seven Mam would take me with her to the Band-of-Hope meeting where she used to play the piano. I loved to listen and afterwards she would promise to arrange piano lessons for me. She was true to her word and in January 1944 I started having piano and later organ lessons. I took to it like a duck to water and the rest as they say is history. My family roots run deep and wide in Llanelli and there are countless names that paved the way for my appearance as a new-born in the Hick Street house that is, after all these years, still my home. I can trace my family down the generations on both my mother's and my father's side with links to almost every corner of the town though sadly, surviving relatives grow fewer with the passing of the years.

Among those still with us is my cousin Rev. David Hughes Jones who since 1949 has pursued a long and successful journey of gospel ministry with the help of his wife Meirys. This capable and wise lady was an excellent mainstay throughout his career and like a sister to me. David rose to the highest rank of Welsh preacher, and his services were much in demand all over Wales. He is also an excellent poet, and has written and

My supportive cousin, Rev. David Hughes Jones and his wife Meirys.

published the excellent volume of Welsh poetry and hymns titled O'r Haul a'r Heli — From the Sun and Foam.

Other surviving relatives are my closest cousin Dilys who I have relied on more than anyone since Mam's death. Sadly, her sister May died just a short time ago. In their younger days they were inseparable, even marrying two brothers — Willie and Gwilym Williams. Dilys and her husband Gwilym ran what was Machynys Fach Farm while May and Willie farmed Machynys Fawr. My mother was born in that area too and because of these strong links when I had the honour to become a member of the Gorsedd in 1964 I chose Machynys as my Bardic name. Finally, with a hint that parts of our family may boast some degree of longevity there are my cousins Annie — the oldest living member of my family — who celebrates her centenary on August 8, this year, her sister Amelia, 90, and several others who are between 73 and 85 years of age — Joan Quan, from Guildford whose own mother lived until she was 98; brother and sister Glan and Rhianon, who live in Dafen; Melville and Lety Tonge, Llwynhendy; Betty Burnhill, Pennard; Barbara Sharrard, Swiss Valley, Llanelli; her sister Bethan Evans who lives in Caldicot together with Geraint and Nancy Griffiths of Solihull. Other cousins include Richard Christopher who is the conductor of Northampton Male Voice Choir and his sister Anna Lintott whose mother Marian was very close to my own. They shared an interest in acting and often performed together. Last but by no means least is Patricia Walker.

Family, friends and personalities known well both locally and nationally figure largely in recollections that follow and I hope their recall will be as much a source of enjoyment for those whose memory of them will be refreshed as it is for those who never made their acquaintance. On this count and perhaps with more serious intention my memories may help record the existence of some of these people. It has certainly been a privilege to share my life with them all.

Dilys and May, enjoying one of the holidays they shared.

In Concert
Fun, friends and funds

Setting up a concert party in an attempt to raise funds for a needy charity was one thing — marvelling as that same group passed its 50th anniversary was quite another, but that, remarkably, is exactly what happened.

One of my teacher's at Llanelli Boys' Grammar School, Mr J Afan Jones sparked the concert party idea. His wife Holly was a member of the Ladies Committee for the Llanelli Blind which diligently organised a monthly tea and entertainment. When I was in the school's sixth form he asked me if I would gather a few of the younger boys and some older acquaintances from Triniti Chapel and put on a show at this regular event.

The debut of what became known as the Gethin Hughes Concert Party was meant to be a one-off event, but was so well received that requests poured in to make it a regular

All set for a sing-song at the piano with some of those who became the backbone, for many years, of the Gethin Hughes concert party.

15

All smiles from Joy Davies, Michael Thomas and Daphne Edwards during a comedy concert party routine entitled The Banjo, The Flute and The Violin.

feature of Llanelli's entertainment calendar. As the years passed the number of performances grew reaching more than 1,300 concerts in venues across Wales, all helping to raise funds for a variety of charities, organisations and good causes.

The concert party delighted audiences with a selection of old time favourites, music hall renditions and comedy sketches provided by a dedicated team accompanied by myself on the piano. Its first production to achieve major acclaim was The Sound of Music in 1962. That the play was staged at all was an achievement as the musical was then running in London's West End. We were granted permission to perform it in Llanelli on the strict understanding that the only instrument used was a piano. Some music lovers may remember Anne Anthony as Maria, Betty Tovey as Elsa, Eirwyn Aubrey as Captain Von Trapp and Vera Tiley-James as the Mother Abbess.

There have been other memorable performances, but none would have been possible without the support of party members, a number of whom have shared a particularly long association. The longest serving, at 29 years, was Betty Tovey. Betty was born and bred in St. Thomas, Swansea later married Harold Tovey and lived in the Mayals area.

She was for many years a chorus member of the Welsh National Opera where Margaret Moreland, one of its directors, once remarked that she was the prettiest and most elegant lady in the company. While there Betty often took lead solo parts alongside such well known singers as Joan Hammond, Victoria Elliott, Kyra Vayne, Hervey Alan, Rowland

Jones and Walter Midgeley. In the concert party, Betty, who died in 2003, will be remembered for her renditions of the Laughing Song from Die Fliedermauss; Let the Bright Seraphim from Samson and the hymn I Heard The Voice of Jesus. Equally as memorable were her pleasing duets with a mixture of male and female partners. She also often sang in Sunday Serenade with the Morgan Lloyd Orchestra at the Patti Pavilion, Swansea, and appeared in a memorable production of Handel's Messiah by Capel Als Choral Society at the Market Hall, Llanelli. Among those alongside Betty was Jean Sayers, formerly Jean Evans, the daughter of Evans the Baker, in High Street, Llanelli. A former president of Furnace WI, Jean was a concert party member for 27 years and another who delighted audiences with a winning miscellany of popular solos and duets.

Anne Anthony is another who gave long service — 22 years of it. She was for many years also a member of the Cymric Glee Singers conducted by Robert Charles and one of its soloists as well as being one of the founder members of the famous Hywel Girls Choir. In the concert party, Anne took the lead part of Maria in that memorable performance of The Sound of Music and also gave a superb portrayal of Mary in a Welsh Nativity pageant at Lloyd Street Chapel.

Just a year behind Anne in this length of service roll call is Elwyn Harries, a member of the concert party for 21 years. Elwyn was also a member of the chorus of the Welsh National Opera Company and often sang minor roles there. A stalwart with Llanelli Operatic Society he often sang too, for Burry Port Opera Company. For years Elwyn's rich bass baritone voice and bubbly personality was often called upon to sing in opera and oratorio all over Wales.

Daphne Edwards has 21 years concert party service to her credit. Like many of the other members she could lay claim to wide-ranging musical experience. A long-time member of Cor Glandulais she sang in a concert at St David's Cathedral on March 1, 1993 and also appeared on S4C's Heno programme. When Neil Kinnock was Leader of the Opposition, Daphne sang in the Labour Party Conference in Brighton including a duet with the politician. She has also sung lead parts with both Burry Port and Llanelli operatic societies. Daphne has been privileged to sing duets with some of the world's greatest singers including Forbes Robinson, Arthur Davies, Ryland Davies, Terence Sharpe and Janet Coster. For three years she was a regular soloist with the Noson Lawen held at Craig y Nos Castle in the Swansea Valley. In the concert party Daphne delighted audiences with numbers including Russalka's Song to the Moon, Cymru Fach and Love's Garden of Roses.

Like Daphne, Joy Davies, originally from Llangennech, was a member of the party for 21 years and both coincidentally were educated at Llanelli Girls' Grammar School. Joy still lives in Llangennech and is a deacon and Sunday school teacher at Bethesda Chapel

The cast of The Sound of Music, the concert party's first success, in 1962.

there. Three years ago she sang solos on S4C's popular Dechrau Canu, Dechrau Canmol programme. An excellent soprano, Joy is a member of Cor Glandulais with whom she often sings solos. Joy is yet another who has sung with well known singers, among them Arthur Davies, Ryland Davies and Terence Sharp. Richard Rees, the well known Blue Riband bass baritone, described her as one of the sweetest soprano voices he had ever heard — a high tribute indeed. Joy has taken lead roles with both Llanelli and Penyrheol operatic societies. Her contribution to the concert party was tremendous and her popular songs were Two Operatic Sopranos with Betty Tovey; Manly Heart with Elwyn Harries and Holy Spirit with Janet Williams.

Hugh Davies was for many years the oldest member of the concert party, but in his late seventies looked years younger. His lyrical tenor voice was as fresh then as it would surely have been 50 years before. Hugh was a member of the concert party for 19 years and although in later times devoted a great deal of his time to caring for his wife Myfanwy he still found time to delight audiences with songs that included Elen Fwyn and If With All Your Heart from Elijah.

Janet Williams came from a family of songsters. Her mother May was a beautiful soloist as were two of her brothers and her sister. Items she made hers in 18 years with the party included Charming Chloe, Llansteffan and Over the Rainbow.

For eight years the rich contralto voice of Ann Thomas, who played leads with Llanelli Operatic Society and aided the chorus of the Burry Port Opera, delighted audiences with solos I'll Walk Beside You, Home Sweet Home and Into Thy Hands as well as duets such as Evening Prayer with Janet Williams and Summer Has Come with Daphne Edwards. Ann was another one time member of the Hywel Girls Choir.

Gethin Hughes with members of his concert party at a civic reception at Llanelli's Mayor's parlour to commemorate the group's 25th anniversary.

Phillip Hooper was involved with the concert party for around six years. He and wife Myra have two sons — John and Paul. Both are brilliant instrumentalists — John, a first class violinist, was Llanelli Young Musician of the Year in 1992 and Paul is an excellent trombone player. Some of Phillip's audience pleasers were Friend of Mine and Hole in My Bucket with Ann Thomas and Waitress, Porter and Upstairs Maid sung with Ann Thomas and Jean Sayers.

Others who contributed to the concert party's half century of entertainment and fund-raising, included Tydfil Morgan, violin; Jenny Thomas and John Griffiths, comedy duets; Annie Vaughan, soprano; Vilna Challenor, contralto; Tom Rees, baritone; Eddie Watkeys, tenor; James Herbert, tenor; Raymond May, tenor; Gertie Bowen, soprano; and Elsie Jones, Florence Griffiths, Liz Meredith and Ruth Bonnell, all chorus members; Fraser Morris and Meiriona J Rees, Welsh recitations; Blodwen Morris, Betty Jenkins, Edwina Barney, Nan Herbert, Vera Tiley-James, Frank Herbert, Eirwyn Aubrey, Meirion Rees, Iwan Rees, Gillian Rees, Dennis Jones, Jeffrey Hobbs, Lynne Richards, Peggy Williams. David Griffiths, baritone, Llannon; John Williams tenor; Givlyn Evans, Tom Evans (Gwanas) and Wendy Hewitt, Burry Port, also provided invaluable assistance.

Others who many will remember included Mary Williams, of Upper Mill, who was with the party for 26 years and sang until she was 84. The popular solo she made her own was Smiling Throu'. There was also Gertie Tiley, mother of Vera Tiley-James, who in addition to her rendition of the comedy song Maggie, was also a first-class needlewoman, creating many costumes for various productions. Then there was the excellent mother and daughter act of Margaret Lewis who had a lovely soprano voice and her daughter Ann who performed many delightful duet and cameo items. Twins John and Robert Edwards won over many audiences with novelty numbers such as Me and My Teddy Bear, Ship Ahoy and The Changing of the Guard; Glan Jeffreys, Royston Jones, Irene Thomas, Gwyn Richards, Gwen Thomas, Iestyn Harry, Olive Brenton, Gaynor Francis, Hedley Bowen, Ken and Margaret Skinner and David Edwards are the names of others whose talents helped make so many concerts such a success.

The involvement of all of these people brought enjoyment to thousands and helped provide much needed support to a variety of charities. As with the many other characters and personalities who feature on following pages — of local, national and world-wide acclaim — they will all linger long in my memory. Sadly many have passed away, but all have certainly left their mark on me — and Llanelli too in many cases! Their mention here is a salute to their unstinting efforts for their community and beyond.

Sadly, just six weeks after celebrating it's half century in 2004, it was decided to bring down the curtain for the final time on what many have suggested must surely rank among the longest-lived and most successful charity concert parties of all time. It is still missed and mourned by many.

Sir Malcolm Sargent — a true gentleman.

Flash Harry

Manners maketh man

I came to know Sir Malcolm Sargent in 1961 when he became patron of the Llanelli fund raising committee for the 1962 National Eisteddfod of Wales which was held in the town. He was kind and generous, and even invited myself and two of my young music pupils to a Promenade concert rehearsal at the Royal College of Organists along with coffee afterwards at his exclusive Royal Albert Hall Mansions apartment.

It was Tuesday evening in August and Sir Malcolm was rehearsing for a concert at the Royal Albert Hall two days later. We were met at the door of the Royal College of Organists by his chief secretary, Sylvia Darley, a charming lady who showed us to our balcony seats and stayed throughout the rehearsal explaining everything as the evening progressed. Sir Malcolm had under his baton the combined talents of the BBC Symphony Orchestra, Choral Society and Chorus, Hammersmith Choral Society, Welwyn Garden Choral Society together with the London Welsh Choral Society — all in all a total of about 400 voices tackling Mozart's Choral Symphony in G minor.

Sir Malcolm was fully aware that most of them were amateur singers, who had spent the day working in shops, offices or factories, and their only reason for singing was a sheer love of music. I have never seen anything quite like it in all my life — he was a king among musicians teaching not simply music, but a marvellous lesson in manners at the same time exhibiting kindness, diplomacy and yet, alongside that, an ample firmness to achieve the desired result.

He began with the words: "Thank you all for attending the rehearsal this evening. I realise most of you have been on your feet since six o'clock this morning, so I'll try not to prolong matters." The rehearsal proceeded smoothly, with Sir Malcolm occasionally stopping to speak to the gathering. Once he said: "That was very good sopranos, but do you think you could sing it a little quicker and lighter. I think it could possibly sound better. Shall we try it?" Then after repeating that particular passage he stopped again and said: "Well done sopranos, that was excellent. Thank you very much — first class." By this time the sopranos felt as important as the greatest prima donnas in Covent Garden.

As the rehearsal progressed each of the accompanying sections were given similar treatment to draw the very best out of them. To the contraltos he suggested that they glide a certain passage instead of being "choppy", then followed the praise when they dutifully obeyed. The bass section was politely requested to restrain their "rich, mellow voices" just a shade and the tenors coaxed to increase their silvered tone slightly. "I think the blend and harmony might then sound more balanced," said Sir Malcolm. Again the voices responded and the appreciation flowed. He also turned to the orchestra on one occasion and to the strings directed: "You are producing a beautiful tone tonight — fantastic — but perhaps the pizzicato could be a little crisper. Shall we try it?" Before the end of the evening he had made all members of both choir and orchestra feel like a million dollars, and had them eating out of his hand. What a master — the end product was amazing

After the rehearsal Sylvia Darley took us across to Sir Malcolm's flat. Eventually the maestro himself made an appearance clad in his rehearsal rigout — grey pinstripe suit, white shirt, red tie and red carnation. His concert uniform was evening suit, white bow tie and white carnation. People loved and adored him and after meeting him over coffee in his flat I can fully understand why. Affectionately known by the Promenaders as Flash Harry he was also known in musical circles as the man with the white carnation. I was fascinated in his jovial company by his beautiful, lyrical voice, his humility and kindness. He assured me that he loved the Welsh people and the Welsh language and as if to confirm this added : "One of the greatest pieces of music ever written was by a Welshman." I quickly inquired which one that was. His reply, fired off like a bullet from a gun, was: "The Welsh hymn tune Aberystwyth by Dr. Joseph Parry — truly magnificent and what a climax on the seventh line of the hymn, par excellence." He then thanked us for coming and told us to give his love to Wales.

Sir Malcolm was also a patron of the British and Foreign Bible Society and occasionally preached or gave addresses. He was a truly remarkable man — what a musical genius, what a gentleman! One of my most treasured possessions is the autographed photograph he gave me before we left his flat.

Ceridwen Lloyd-Davies in 1957, surrounded by members of the Trinity College Orchestral Society including a young Gethin Hughes, third from the left at the back.

Initial Impression
Ceridwen Lloyd-Davies

The initials CLLD meant only one thing to students of Trinity College, Carmarthen, in 1955 — their champion, Mrs Ceridwen Lloyd-Davies, head of the music department. Ceridwen was born in Griffithstown, Monmouthshire, sister of one Dr Ellis LLoyd, former headmaster of Bishop Gore Grammar School, Swansea, and cousin to well-known violinist Morgan Lloyd. When she married the Rev. Gwilym Davies, she became known as Ceridwen Lloyd-Davies.

Ceridwen was lecturer at St. Mary's College, Bangor, Coleg Harlech and finally at Trinity College, Carmarthen where her son, David Ffrangon Lloyd-Davies became head of the history department and for a short period both mother and son were both lecturers there. Ceridwen was a fine composer, arranger, conductor, accompanist and organist as well as one of Wales's greatest musical adjudicators — officiating in this capacity at the Royal National Eisteddfod of Wales for 30 consecutive years. She was a long-serving examiner for the Welsh Joint Examination Committee, visiting grammar schools all over Wales to officiate over practical music tests.

If, as students, we had a grievance it was off to see dear Ceridwen who would act as mediator between us and the principal. She would say to him: "But Reverend Principal I do not agree with your decision. I think the students have a point." Nine times out of 10 the principal would give in, saying: "Well if you think so Mrs Lloyd-Davies, I'd better reconsider my decision." I remember her as being very simply dressed — plain skirts, woollen jumpers and cardigans in the winter; plain blouses in the summer, flat shoes, fishnet stockings, no make-up and plain, combed hair. No frills. But if she was plain in dress, she was certainly elaborate and ornate in character with a dynamic personality and generous heart. She may have been as straight as a die with a good sense of humour, but Ceridwen Lloyd-Davies also had eyes that could look straight through you if the need or the occasion justified. I owe her so very much. She made me what I am today. I was a young nervous 19-year-old from Llanelli Boys Grammar School with a letter of introduction from Mr Frank Phillips to 'My friend Ceridwen', but when we met she immediately took to me and I to her. What a lady.

Within a month she made me give a talk to second-year students. She insisted I talk in the college chapel on how the pipe organ works — stops, keys, pipes and pedals. The length of the lecture was 55 minutes. I had struggled through to talk for 40 minutes and was about to dry up when, from the back of the chapel, full of tact and wisdom, came the voice of Ceridwen Lloyd-Davies: "That's simply great Mr Hughes, now would you

Ceridwen Lloyd-Davies in classic teaching pose with a group of Trinity College, Carmarthen, music students, in the early 1960s.

kindly demonstrate by playing a few pieces on the pipe organ." What a relief, what a wise lady! She conquered my shyness and nervousness. After that I could talk in front of the Queen, the Prime Minister, the Archbishop of Canterbury — or all three at the same time.

She would always speak near-perfect Welsh apart from a few words. There is a double meaning for pwdr in Welsh — the usual translation, powder and the other meaning is a slang version for laziness or rotten. Once, Ceridwen was adjudicating the 18-25 contralto solo at the 1954 Royal National Eisteddfod in Ystradgynlais. The test piece was Schubert's Who is Sylvia? which has three verses. She gave her adjudication in Welsh and praised one competitor for her rich contralto voice and intelligent phrasing, but she stated that the person was "Pwdwr iawn — chi dim ond canu un pennill. Mae'n rhaid canu y tri pennill." which translates as "You are very lazy — only singing one verse. You must sing the three verses." She never threw her adjectives away. If she said you were good, then you were excellent.

The former Bishop of St David's the Rev. JR Richards, once said: "Ceridwen Lloyd-Davies is a wizard. She could draw music out of a stone. She is pure magic." One of my clearest memories serves to show that he was probably right. She had asked me to play the organ in St David's Cathedral one Sunday in March, 1958. I was then at Halfway County Primary School in my first year of teaching having left college just eight months previously and was nothing if not a little nervous at the musical prospect. Offering reassurance to allay that uncertainty Ceridwen, who passed away in 1989, said: "Don't worry dear, we'll be down there by 10.50am and you'll have 10 minutes to try the organ before the service at 11am. You'll do it well, truly magnificently. You'll be fine. I have great confidence in you."

Knowing that you had CLLD's confidence, you could do almost anything. What a privilege for me to be taught by such a great lady.

Ceridwen Lloyd-Davies at the piano rehearsing with a group of Trinity College students for a special choral performance in 1963.

Electric Example
Betty Tovey

It was in 1947 that I first saw Betty Tovey — on stage at the former Llanelli Public Hall. She was in the dramatised version of Handel's Messiah under the musical direction of Dr. Haydn Morris and production of Emlyn Davies. It was the third work that Capel Als Choral Society had undertaken — the others being Mendelssohn's Elijah and Handel's Samson. Messiah was a far greater challenge for Capel Als than the other two, but the result was a resounding success in which Betty Tovey's performance was superb. Her singing of Rejoice and I Know That My Redeemer Liveth were among the highlights. Her beautiful, lyrical soprano voice soared out with joy and sincerity and her vivacious personality dominated all around her. Also taking part on that memorable occasion were Lynne Richards, Tycroes, contralto; Harding Jenkins, Llwynhendy, bass, and Euryl Coslett, Llangennech, the tenor.

The next time I saw Betty Tovey was four years later on the stage of the Empire Theatre, Swansea, in a production of Verdi's La Traviata by the Welsh National Opera. She was singing the role of Flora. The world famous soprano Heather Harper was singing Violetta. My mother and Auntie Gertie were with me and both wanted to know who the pretty, blonde singer with the enchanting smile and exquisite, mauve evening gown in Act I was. She was of course none other than the same Betty Tovey we had all seen in Llanelli in that memorable Messiah four years earlier.

The South Wales Evening Post critic of the time reported: "Betty Tovey in the minor role of Flora, electrified the stage and stole the show." What a compliment to a lovely woman, a wonderful singer and a superb artist and trouper. Years later, in 1962, I was introduced to Betty by Miss SW Scully, music teacher of Stebonheath Girls' School, and we became long-time close friends. Betty and her husband Harold were also friends with my parents.

Some years later I asked Betty to join my concert party, and she was a faithful member for nearly three decades during which we performed more than 400 concerts together. Her singing of One Fine Day, the Laughing Song from Die Fledermaus and Villia from the Merry Widow were legendary and her vivacious personality, good looks and friendly charm always won rapturous applause from the audience. Betty still took an active part in the concert party up to the age of 80, but singing lighter solos. She also sang at St David's Cathedral and was noted for singing the hymn I Heard The Voice of Jesus Say. I remember when she sang it so beautifully in Moriah Chapel for the Zenana Baptist Movement many in the audience were moved to tears. Betty's first major production with the concert party was in the role of Elsa Schraedar in our Sound of Music production. Six years later she sang again at the Market Hall, this time as Maria Klomp in Holiday In Holland, an original new musical by Meiriona J Rees and myself. Betty added to her credits when she sung The Duchess of Plaza Torre in The Gondoliers in 1981, the first production by Llanelli Amateur Operatic Society.

Some years ago I was invited to a garden party at Buckingham Palace in recognition of 30 years charity work in the Llanelli area. My mother was invited too, but ill-health prevented her from attending so Betty accompanied me in her place and we both enjoyed the experience very much. We had lunch at the Savoy Hotel — a gift to us both from Mam — before taking a taxi to Buckingham Palace where we met both the Queen and the Prince of Wales. Betty remained one of my closest friends until her death in October, 2003. On one occasion with another friend, Sybil Perrot, we enjoyed a brief holiday to Eastbourne. While there we visited Elsie Waters — one half of the great music hall pairing of Elsie and Doris Waters. Elsie sung a song for us, which she and her sister Doris had composed, and she presented a copy of it to Betty, a long-time vice-president of Llanelli Young Music Lovers' Association to which she gave 100 per cent support in carol festivals, concerts and panel games.

Together with her family she had many friends in Llanelli, and on many occasions we were entertained to scrumptious meals at her homes, first of all in the Mayals, Swansea and later Bishopston, Gower. She was an expert with cream slices and chocolate eclairs!

Myself, accompanied by Betty Tovey, after attending a Garden Party at Buckingham Palace.

Spirit Raiser
Gracie Fields

One of the biggest stars of the last century was that much-loved lassie from Lancashire, Gracie Fields. Our Gracie as she was affectionately known was a film star, cabaret star, music-hall star, as well as a delightful television and radio personality.

Gracie Fields was a superb artist who would have the audience eating out of her hand. Her unique voice had a vast range. She could sing coloratura solos like The Laughing Song and the Doll Song with consumate ease and beautiful religious and sacred solos like The Holy City, The Lord's Prayer, Ave Maria, Lost Chord and Bless This House with such conviction and feeling that she brought tears to many eyes. At other times they would have been tears of joy and mirth for her comedy items — The Biggest Aspidestra In The World, Walter, My Little Bottom Drawer, I Took My Harp To A Party, Never Cried So Much In All My Life — were real gems and nobody but Gracie Fields could put them over so well.

Her memorable Second World War film with its theme song Sing As We Go was Let The People Sing while her two other famous wartime songs were Wish Me Luck and Now Is The Hour. Others she immortalised were McNamara's Band, How Are Things In Glockemora, Somewhere Over The Rainbow and of course Sally. Gracie was born in Rochdale and worked in the cotton mills until she was discovered by her first husband Archie Pitt, who became her agent, though the marriage only lasted three years. Her second marriage was to Monty Banks, a millionaire who lived on the Isle of Capri in Italy. Gracie moved there and the couple remained together for 18 years until he died in 1949. In 1953 she fell in love with a radio mechanic — Boris — who came to mend her radio. They were married for 28 years until her death in 1981 at the age of 83.

Gracie Fields did a great deal of charity work throughout her life, and entertained thousands of troops during the Second World War with forces entertainment group ENSA. A number of Llanelli people were also involved with the organisation including Tom Rees and Meurig Price. They often spoke of the charm, kindness and humility of Gracie Fields and how she liked seeing people and chatting to them. Megan Holliday — formerly Megan Thomas of Llwynhendy — who now lives in Birmingham also recalled her ENSA days in Italy and India. She said Gracie was a lovely person who would encourage her and her fellow Welsh girls on stage or coax them in the street to burst into a chorus of Sing As We Go. Oliver Brenton from Gorseinon often spoke of the entertainer's artistry, and recalled one concert when Gracie captivated the audience with a superb performance of Pedro the Fisherman. I was fortunate to meet up with Gracie

Fields in 1962 at her beautiful home, Canzone del Mare on the Isle of Capri while on a coach tour. Some friends were always keen for a sing-song and did so on spotting a piano while we were dining in Gracie's restaurant. Eventually I went over to it and couldn't resist playing The Biggest Aspidestra in the World. Suddenly, the star herself appeared and started singing along to what was one of her most famous songs.

When we had finished she thanked me for playing it, and we became firm friends, and remained so until her death. I regularly received a Christmas card from her, and often a gift — always signed Gracie and Boris. When the Queen honoured her in 1981 with the DBE, she sent me a signed photograph of herself in a beautiful evening gown on which she had written: "To Gethin, from the Old — New Dame Gracie Fields." She was thrilled to receive the honour, but only lived for a short time afterwards.

Gracie Fields — a superb entertainer who would have the audience eating out of her hand.

Her pianist for many years was Harry Parr Davies from Neath. He also composed many of her songs including Pedro the Fisherman, so when Gracie realised I was Welsh and that Neath was quite near Llanelli it quickly strengthened our friendship. I shall always remember this great lady's kindness and treasure a signed copy of her autobiography which she gave to me. I frequently perform The Biggest Aspidestra in the World, as a special concert tribute to one of our greatest and brightest stars. I have even performed a Welsh translation of it achieved by my cousin, Rev. David Hughes Jones of Rhyl, on S4C's Heno programme. Gracie's popularity is evidenced by the fact that for many her memory lingered, not as Dame Gracie but simply Our Gracie.

Wake-up Call
Loti Rees-Hughes

Travelling home from Oslo, Norway on a North Sea ferry during August 1965 I shared a table with a family from Newcastle upon Tyne. I soon realised that I was speaking to none other than Ed Milne MP for South Shields and Parliamentary Under Secretary for Education, his wife and daughter. When he discovered I hailed from Llanelli he inquired — to my great surprise — if I knew Loti Rees-Hughes. I replied — to his surprise this time — that we were good friends.

He immediately began relating an incident that occurred on Ladies' Day at the Labour Party conference the previous year. He told how the cream of the party's womenfolk were all giving speeches — Edith Summerskill, Barbara Castle, Bessie Braddock, Lady Megan Lloyd George, Jennie Lee, Alice Bacon and Irene White. All were very good, but towards the end of the day proceedings had begun to drag and many delegates were beginning to snooze. This state of affairs was soon brought to an abrupt halt however, when the final speaker of the day took the rostrum. Everyone was woken with a start by an unknown woman representing the constituency Labour Party. She was brilliant, electrifying the conference hall with her eloquence and earning a standing ovation. This dynamic speaker was none other than Llanelli's very own Loti Rees-Hughes. So impressed was Lowe the Daily Herald newspaper cartoonist, that he drew a caricature of her that filled the entire front page of the newspaper. Ed Milne ended his tale with the words: "You know Gethin, Loti Rees-Hughes should be in Parliament." I was very proud to hear him speak so highly of this daughter of Llanelli.

Loti however was no stranger to making her mark with people — whoever they were. When the Duke of Edinburgh opened the new Boys' Grammar School in Pwll in 1960 Alderman W Douglas Hughes was the chairman of governors. His duty was to show the Duke around and introduce him to fellow governors. He was going down the line introducing them when they came to Loti Rees-Hughes. Alderman Hughes introduced her: "Your Royal Highness this is Alderman Mrs Loti Rees-Hughes — who incidentally is my wife." The Duke commented jokingly: "Jobs for the girls is it?" to which Loti, like a flash, replied: "No, by-election Your Royal Highness." What a character she was.

Later, the Duke was sharing refreshments with the headmaster, Stanley G Rees and his wife Connie and he inquired: "Who is this Loti Rees-Hughes. She is superb — she should be in Parliament, she would be excellent in the House of Commons. She would get things moving." What a tribute from the Duke of Edinburgh. Loti was an excellent speaker and a good councillor. Many people will remember a memorable Gymanfa

Loti Rees-Hughes, right, with sisters Casssie and Mati in discusssion with presenter Myfanwy Howel during a television programme.

Ganu in Adulam Chapel, Felinfoel, when she, her two sisters and their uncle took part. David Rees conducted the singing, Cassie accompanied two of her well-known solo pupils on the piano, Mati read from the scriptures and Loti presided over it all in a most excellent manner. And who was lucky enough to be at the organ on that auspicious occasion — me of course!

Many years before, an incident occurred which I will never forget — and not simply because it was my first meeting with Loti. At the time she was married to Islwyn Hopkin, physics teacher at Stebonheath Boys' Secondary Modern School and had a son, Deian. She was also a county councillor and our paths initially crossed at the Llanelli Borough Council elections of 1946. My uncle, John Griffiths, along with Gwilym Thomas and WE Payne, was a Labour candidate. Because of this my mother had asked me to give out leaflets asking people to vote for them. A pal came to help me in the booth at St Paul's School, at the top of Hick Street where we lived and we gave out hundreds of the pamphlets until we had none left. We were enjoying ourselves so much that we decided to carry on giving out leaflets — for the other candidates!

We started with some for Mr J Sidney Jones — an Independent candidate — who was an elder at my chapel, Triniti. Being only 11 years old, I thought it was a good thing to help him until eventually his leaflets came to an end. Then we turned our attention to handing out leaflets for another Independent candidate, Ted Howells — a friend of my father. This we did until these too, ran out. The only ones remaining were for the Communist Party, and as one of the candidates was Ernest Leyshon a brother of Mrs Lily Sims a very devout Christian lady and faithful member of Triniti Chapel, I decided we should help him too and so we started giving leaflets out for the Communist candidates. We had given out loads when we handed one to a woman and asked her to vote for the Communists — it was none other than Councillor Loti Hopkin. She was horrified, and asked me to hand the Communist leaflets over to her saying: "If your Uncle John or your mother knew you were giving out these they would have a stroke." She promptly handed us a fresh pile of Labour Party leaflets.

A month later I met Loti Hopkin again. I had landed up in Stebonheath Boys Secondary Modern School for a year. Mr Islwyn Hopkin the physics teacher was also my form teacher. For a Christmas concert every class was responsible for performing two items. One of ours was a character version of Good King Wenceslas and I was cast as King Wenceslas. Islwyn Hopkin told us that his wife would bring us clothes and a crown for King Wenceslas, and help us to dress. When she arrived it was none other than County Councillor Mrs Loti Hopkin.

Sadly Islwyn Hopkin died in 1950 at the early age of 44, and five years later Loti married Alderman W Douglas Hughes so becoming Loti Rees-Hughes. My last memory of her was at the Royal National Eisteddfod held in Llanelli in 1962. I had worked very hard over the two preceeding years organising functions to raise money for the eisteddfod and had been one of the chief stewards for the week — a thankless task, but at the choral concert on the Saturday, I was privileged to sit in the front row with five very distinguished women: Gwen Morgan, Florence Holloway, Rosa Dickens-Jenkins,Telynores Dyfed; Olwen Williams — and Loti Rees-Hughes.

This final concert of the week was a performance of Verdi's Requiem with the Royal Philharmonic Orchestra, Eisteddfod Choir and well known London artists. It was superb, and Wyn Morris had conducted brilliantly, but refused to sing Hen Wlad Fy Nhadau to close the eisteddfod. The four ladies were enraged at the fact that he had left the stage with no rendition of our National anthem. The orchestra members were already packing their instruments away when suddenly I heard Gwen, Rosa, Florence and Olwen urging: "Go on Loti."

Immediately Loti stood to her feet, climbed onto the stage, asked D Cecil Williams, who was at the organ, to give her an E flat and started to sing and conduct Hen Wlad Fy Nhadau. The response was electric. The 8,000-strong audience stood to their feet and joined in with gusto, repeating the chorus and finally applauding Loti Rees-Hughes for her bravery, her passion for Wales and its culture — and for her loyalty to the Welsh National Anthem. When Loti died at the age of 62 it was a great loss to Llanelli in particular and to Wales in general. I'm very proud to have been associated with this great character and was always delighted to receive her cards sent from all over the world saying simply: "Cofion cynnes Loti!" — Regards from Loti!"

Meiriona J Rees in 1980 at the main door of the chapel she supported so faithfully – Triniti.

Twin Talents

Meiriona J Rees

Ivor and Mattie Rees had five children — Lewis, Meiriona, Aranwen, Nancy and Ifan — and they all carried their mother's maiden name of Jenkins. Mattie was a faithful member of Triniti Chapel, following in her mother's footsteps. Ivor Rees was awarded the Victoria Cross, for bravery in Ypres, Belgium, in the First World War. As a result, Mattie was known in Triniti and in Llanelli's Tyisha district as Mrs Rees, VC and the children were referred to as the VC's.

Meiriona, never married and always preferred to be known as Meiriona J Rees or sometimes as MJR. She was educated at Llanelli County School before studying shorthand and typing in Pagefield. With the advent of the Second World War Meiriona served in the ATS. Afterwards she became a secretary in the offices of Richard Thomas and Baldwins in Machynys, and when the works closed she worked for many years in the Department of Health and Social Security in the town's Stepney Street.

Meiriona was a very talented person, a fluent speaker in both Welsh and English and often preached in the pulpits of various Llanelli chapels. She was also a very good elocutionist and for three years a member of my concert party. Rev. TC Lewis, former minister of Triniti Chapel, once said: "If there were grants and financial help in 1939, Meiriona would have easily won a place in university, achieved her degree and probably have become a successful author."

These joint talents shone brightly in 1966 and 1967 when Meiriona and I collaborated to write a pageant in Welsh — Pasiant Genedigaeth Iesu Grist. Meiriona wrote the script and I the music. It was performed for three nights at Lloyd Street Chapel in December 1966 and December 1967. The producers were the late Minnie Morgan, Labour Exchange, the late Elsie Jones, Welsh mistress at Llanelli Girls' Grammar School, and Dai Smith, former headmaster of Graig Comprehensive School. Dai also took the part of innkeeper and Vera Tiley-James was the innkeeper's wife. Anne Anthony was Mary, John Rees, former deputy headmaster of Ysgol y Strade, Joseph and Raymond Challenor, former headmaster of Bryngwyn Comprehensive School, King Herod.

In May 1967 Meiriona and I joined forces again to write and produce an operetta — Holiday in Holland — which was staged in the Market Hall, Llanelli, with Betty Tovey and Raymond Challenor taking the leads. In earlier years my concert party had performed smaller works by Meiriona — Once Upon A Time and Ahoy There — both at the Parish Hall. I first came to know Meiriona back in 1947 when she was my Sunday

School teacher in Triniti Chapel for over six years. She later became superintendent of the children's Sunday School, a post she held for around 20 years. Both of us were elected elders on the same night in February 1967 and were inducted and ordained in Saron Chapel, Furnace, in April that same year. The time seems to have passed so quickly, but we were also both recipients of an engraved plaque presented by the elders of Triniti to celebrate 25 years among them. Meiriona who died in 1993 was then the chapel secretary and I pulpit secretary, so I had the privilege and pleasure to work with this remarkable and talented lady for a long period of time.

One occasion I remember clearly is when I was asked to play the organ for the first time for Sunday services at Triniti Chapel in November 1954. It was late on a Saturday evening when the organist sent someone to ask me to deputise, and deliver the church and organ keys. It was a filthy night — cold, wet and windy. Mackintosh, wellingtons and umbrella were the order of things before setting off at 10.15pm for Craddock Street, to ask Meiriona to come with me for company to practice the hymns on the organ.

Down we both trudged and arrived at Chapel House at 10.45pm. The caretaker, Jenny Thomas joined Meiriona and myself at the organ, and all three of us remained there until half an hour after midnight — Meiriona and Jenny straining their voices to sing all the hymns with me.

Gathered around the piano during rehearsal for a Llanelli YMCA concert. There was always time to take a break and smile for the camera however.

Rainbow Man
Dr. Clarence Raybould

Dr. Clarence Raybould was for years conductor of the BBC Midland Light Orchestra and assistant to Sir Adrian Boult with the BBC Symphony Orchestra. In 1946 he was appointed the first conductor of the then newly formed National Youth Orchestra of Wales and was affectionately known by many as Dr. Rainbow. He was indeed a very colourful character who I first met with Frank Phillips, Don Preece, Elfed Morgan and Cedric Francis in county orchestra courses held at Trinity College, Carmarthen.

Dr. Raybould would come to the courses to audition young orchestral players for the National Youth Orchestra of Wales and we soon became very good friends. On one of these the course directors — Cedric Francis and Don Preece — with Elfed Morgan's blessing thought it would be a good idea to have someone to entertain orchestras B and C, while orchestra A performed for the public. They asked me to arrange a visit by my concert party on the Wednesday evening and as a result along came eager stalwarts Jenny Thomas, Mary Williams, Vera Tiley-James, Anne Anthony, Gertie Bowen, Betty Tovey and John Griffiths.

The children of Orchestras B and C enjoyed our performance so much that they informed Dr. Raybould of their delight at the end of the public concert. The result was a command performance for him and members of orchestra A at 11pm during which one of the comedy numbers was Un Bys Un Bawd Yn Symud or in English — One Finger, One Thumb, Keeps Moving. The song of course eventually going through to finger, thumb, hand, arm, leg, head, slap on the chest, stand up and down and turn around. All very entertaining for the audience and energetic for the performers. Party member Jenny Thomas coaxed Dr. Raybould onto the stage, taught him the Welsh words and finally he joined us in this humourous song. There was loud applause from the audience and he enjoyed every moment.

Afterwards he promised me that he would return to Llanelli soon. True to his word, this he did. In June 1962, he travelled from his home in Devon for a weekend. His main purpose was to conduct congregational English hymns in a special service at Moriah Baptist Chapel. It was organised by the Bryn-ar-y-mor Ladies Choir. The Welsh hymns were conducted by Elfed Morgan while National Blue Riband soprano Trixie Walters was the soloist. Eirwen Pritchard officiated and I was at the organ. Dr. Raybould was the guest for the weekend of choir president Mrs Jessie John and her husband Gerald in Marsh Street, while we were all invited to tea on the Sunday to the Heol Goffa home of Annie Nicholas and her husband Nick. Dr. Raybould enjoyed every moment and asked

Where every organist should be — at the keyboard. This is me playing in Triniti Chapel.

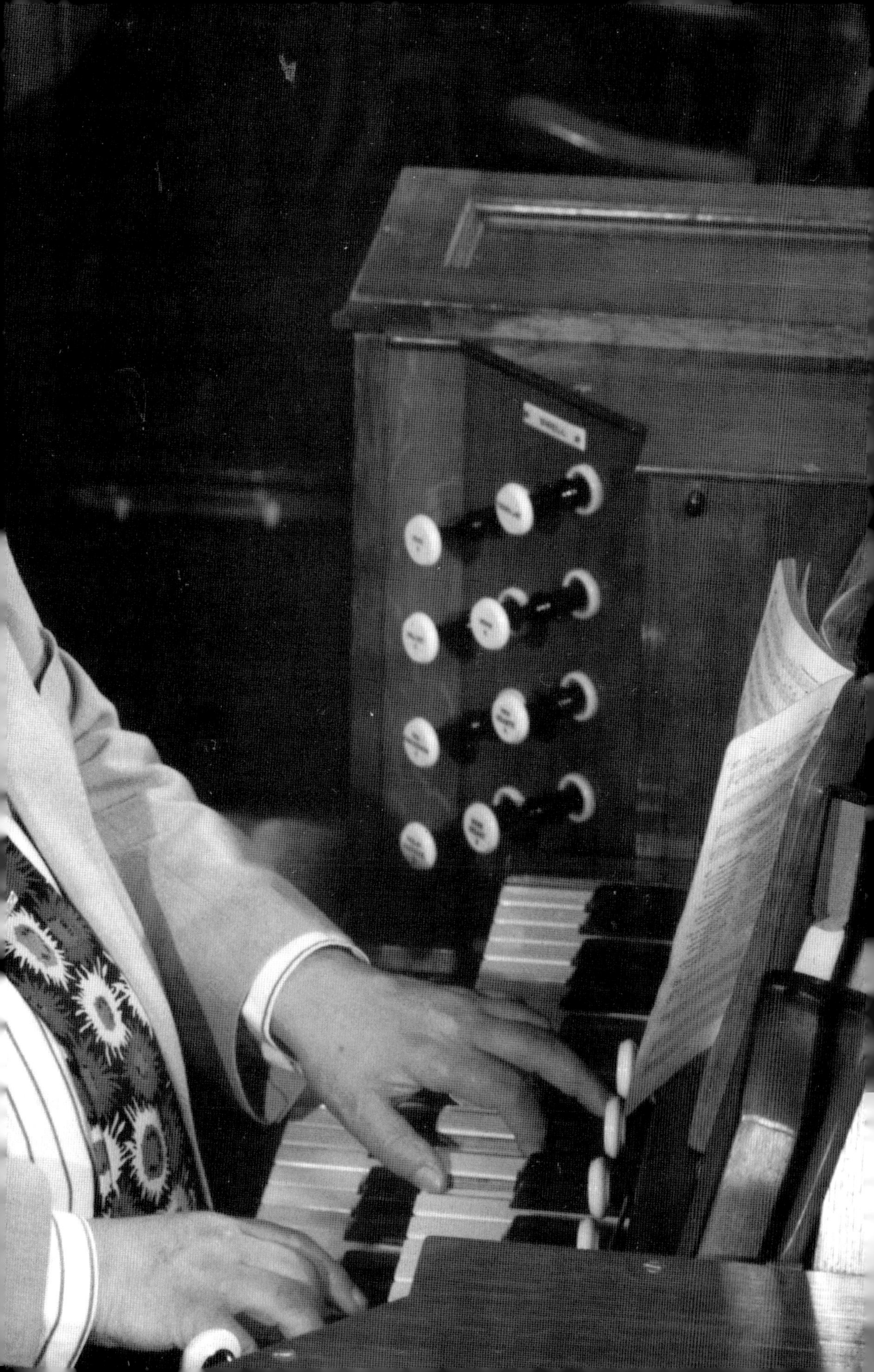

JR Williams — one of the teachers and also great characters that few of those who attended Llanelli Boys' Grammar School in the late 1940s and early 1950s will fail to remember. Below: Huw Roberts, whose teachings were also something to behold.

if he could be granted one very special request. It was to hear the choir sing what he described as one of the best pieces of music ever written — Aberystwyth by Dr. Joseph Parry. How strange to hear almost the exact repetition of the words spoken by Sir Malcolm Sargent during my visit to the Royal Albert Hall a few months earlier. These musical giants certainly appreciated the work of Joseph Parry. And there is no doubt that the musical world saluted their talents too.

Lively Lessons
Some school stalwarts

When I became a pupil at Llanelli Boys' Grammar School in 1946 there were a host of characters on the teaching staff — DT Roberts, WT Stockton, HW Hampton, David Roderick, Frank Phillips and Haydn Jones among them — but none were more popular than Rev. Huw Roberts, JR Williams and J Afan Jones. In that year and those that quickly followed, Huw Bobs and JR — as they were affectionately referred to — in particular reigned supreme as champions of the Gym-Gym or Gymdeithas Gymraeg. They were the Welsh Society.

Huw Roberts came to Llanelli in 1919 as a Welsh teacher at the town's County School. He was also Minister of Emmanuel Baptist Chapel for three years. He and his wife Maude made their home in Marble Hall Road — opposite the school which later became the Boys' Grammar. He often filled the pulpits of the town on a Sunday — Welsh or English. Whenever the chance came to preach the Gospel he took it. But he also lived what he preached and was a devout and sincere Christian. This shone through his character as a teacher in the grammar school — pupils loved Huw Bobs. He was one of us. He loved Wales and his passion for its language and culture was unsurpassed. He was like a flame burning. He was on fire for the Welsh language, but was never narrow or petty-minded; never rude to English people. He taught his wife Maude Welsh and hundreds of children besides. He would come into the class, and ask every boy for a halfpenny, holding out his hand out and asking "Dewch a dime i mi" — give me a halfpenny. Everyone would give him a halfpenny once a week and as a result he collected thousands of halfpennies and converted them into pounds to start and build a Welsh and scripture library in the school.

It was customary for Huw Roberts to open the season of the Gym-Gym with a spirited address, and also give a wonderful St David's Day talk on famous Welshmen. This tradition was carried on for many years after he retired until he was 88. He lived to the ripe old age of 95.

We would have lots of fun with him in his lessons. He would poke innocent fun at some of the other teachers such as Mr David Roderick who was six foot tall and always hitting his head on the chemistry lab door, or Mr Stockton eating toast and honey for breakfast and the honey would stick to his moustache. The head of English was Mr HW Hampton whose graduate gown was torn and tattered. Mr Roberts would say: "Mr Hampton was having a snooze on the couch at home when his gown caught fire, and he was shouting fire! fire! and Mrs Hampton had to throw a bucket of water over the gown, that's why it is in ribbons." He would comment that "Mr Glyn Hughes has come to school riding his iron horse." It was of course a bicycle.

What a character he was — brilliant at teaching Welsh grammar. He told us about the 'i dot' and 'u bedol' — the short and sharp i with a dot, and the long and drawn out u with a cup— he was a master. He often addressed chapel societies and his great lecture was about Capelilo an old Welsh tramp who had a religious experience. He was a brilliant orator, excellent teacher, and superb preacher. One of his great sermons was "The Lord's Prayer — Our Father — God a father to all who believe." He loved everything Welsh and worked endlessly for the Urdd movement, Plaid Cymru, the Cymrodorion, Baptist Union, Free Church Council, the Ecumenical movement and for Bethania Baptist Chapel. In 1948-49 when I was in Form III, Huw Roberts used to take both the upper and lower sixth forms in advanced Welsh. On a Thursday afternoon they had three lessons in the second of which I used to have history with Mr Frank Phillips. Now Huw Roberts knew this, and as he and Frank were good friends, he used to send some of the sixth formers to fetch me. I was press-ganged every week, sometimes dragged, sometimes carried, but always taken up to the physics lab where Huw Roberts taught his Welsh classes, to perform a favourite impersonation of Dorothy Squires singing At the End of the Day. Mr Roberts placed me every week on top of a bench and there I had to perform. When I came to the line "Carry them high, when they seem to be low," he and his pupils would have tears streaming down their faces. That was their five-minutes of comic relief in the middle of Welsh literature and poetry. I doubt whether Huw Roberts had even heard of Dorothy Squires. All he would say in Welsh every Thursday was: "Get up on the bench and do that woman." Throughout his period at the grammar school until he retired in July 1949, Rev. Huw Roberts always took the Welsh assemblies, and the headmaster Mr TV Shaw would always take the English ones. For my first two years there I was in Junior assembly in the general science lab so I only had the chance to hear Mr Roberts take the Welsh assemblies for one year before he retired, but they are unforgettable memories. His services were excellent.

Meanwhile Dickie Spitfire was the nickname accorded to Mr J Ryland Williams because he was always on the go, never resting, always working or rushing around. He joined the staff of Llanelli County School in 1940 and remained there until he retired in 1971. At first he was in the Welsh department, but in 1960 was made head of history, ending his illustrious career as deputy headmaster. We all loved JR. He travelled from Carmarthen to Llanelli daily by train, and loved it when some of us boys would carry his bag, and send him to the train. He would treat us to a cup of tea and a cake in Allegri's Cafe and would love to chat. One of the waitresses who often served us was Gwen Evans of Felinfoel, widow of the Rev. Clifford Evans. It was JR who deputised for Rev. Huw Roberts and also his successor Rev. Robert Wynne, to take the Welsh Assemblies. With a lovely tenor voice, JR was given the job of pitching the hymns during the Welsh assemblies as there was no piano in the general science lab. He did a fine job of things — he would sing the first line and the boys would then join in. JR's services were excellent. He was very dramatic in his readings, particularly superb at play reading. He would depict and impersonate all the characters, and one of the highlights of the Welsh Society's season was the evening when JR Williams would read a play. I shall never forget his junior Welsh lessons. He used to read to us from Cymru'r Plant (The Children's Wales). One story I shall always remember was the Eagle and Whimpy Brown — very dramatic. Later, in Form V, his poetry readings were superb and his analysis of Welsh novels masterpieces. He brought the characters alive in front of our eyes. At one time he took some English lessons with similar fervour and his geography lessons on The Americas were also something to think about.

With the English play JR Williams gave the public never-to-be-forgotten productions of Strife, Good Friday, Murder at the Cathedral, Dr. Faustus and Macbeth. He was as at home in Shakespeare as he was in Welsh comedy. JR Williams also loved to take part with pupils in Welsh Noson Lawen which we took around many chapel vestries — Bethania, Calfaria, Moriah, Capel Als and Tabernacl as well as Adulam, Felinfoel. After these we would send him to the train — the 9.30pm, from Llanelli. He was devoted to his pupils and his teaching. He lived for, and loved, every moment. He also organised fabulous school trips. My first was in Form One — I was the only first former involved as it was meant to be forms four to six, but the senior boys persuaded JR to let me go. We went to Cardiff and Roath Park lake, and onto the rowing boats there. I remember JR shouting to the senior boys in Welsh: "Look after that child and watch he doesn't fall in the lake."

Another of our favourites was John Afan Jones who had a remarkable record to his credit — he taught at Llanelli Boys' Grammar School for 43 years. He started as a PT teacher in 1914 under its first headmaster, William Lewis. By the time I reached the school in 1947, Mr Afan Jones was head of Latin, and took us four times a week — on Tuesday mornings, Wednesday afternoons, Friday mornings and then again in the afternoons. It was a tough dose for both teacher and pupil to have four Latin lessons a week so by Friday afternoon we were all cheesed off, and Afan — as he was affectionately known — was aware of this. So in that lesson he would beckon me to the front of the class with five or six others and instruct us to perform a Welsh sketch or drama.

John Afan Jones — a grammar school stalwart.

His great love was drama — both acting and producing. Afan Jones had a wonderful sense of humour and would often tease us and we in turn would do the same. We had our lessons in the old red hut and if it was raining on the walk there he would pull his gown up over his head and look exactly like a Nun. The boys would shout within

45

Me, front left, with some fellow grammar school pupils, JR Williams and Welsh teacher Glyn Hughes in the late 1940s. Below: Yvonne Watkin-Rees.

hearing — "Here comes Mother Afana." He would laugh at the comment and take it all in good part. In those days an annual drama competition was held in the school. When we were in Form 1 he encouraged us to put on a sketch. The name of our play was The Three Coloured Cat. It was a shambles made up as we went along so that when we next performed it there were many differences in the script. Afan Jones knew this, and purposely put us through to the finals against Form IV and Form VI. We couldn't have been too bad as we ended up sharing first prize.

In 1960 I temporarily found myself on the staff of the Boys' Grammar School. Three of my closest friends there were JR, Harding Rees who later became a lecturer at Barry College, and Denis Jones, later headmaster and then at Ysgol Gyfun y Graig. JR would often treat Denis, Harding and myself to a meal and in later years Blodwen, Denis's mother would invite JR and myself to tea on his birthday. What a welcome we'd have in their Elgin Road home. My last memory of JR, who died when he was 71, was at his home in Priory Street, Carmarthen. For six years after he retired. I would go down a few times a year on the train to see him and his wife Esta. I used to enjoy these visits very much. JR would want all the news about Llanelli, my work and travels.

Yvonne Watkin-Rees will be remembered by many as the first woman on the staff and for the pupils at least something of as novelty. An Ammanford girl she came to the school each Thursday to teach speech therapy and drama. The boys all loved her and fought to help carry her bag and her books. Yvonne trained at the Royal Academy and was a brilliant actress, once taking the role of Lady Bracknell in The Importance Of Being Earnest at the Grand Theatre, with Swansea Little Theatre. She was brilliant with dialects – unbeatable — and often took an evening of recitation, perhaps an excerpt from Under Milk Wood where she would take on each of the characters in turn. She also loved some of the Welsh humour.

Perfect Harmony

Mattie Bateman-Morris

Without a doubt Mattie Bateman-Morris was one of the best known and most popular characters in Llanelli. She was born Audrey Martha as the only child of David and May Bateman of Auckland Terrace, now Tunnel Road, but since she was a month old was known as Mattie.

Her parents were staunch members of Moriah Baptist Chapel until their deaths but, at the age of four, Mattie went with friends to St Alban's Church — and there she remained. In 1942 she was appointed deputy organist there. The organist at the time was Joyce Whittaker and the choirmaster was Leslie Morris. Three years later in 1945 at the age of just 19, Mattie was appointed organist and in 1947 she married the choirmaster, Leslie Morris so becoming Mattie Bateman-Morris.

Mattie's piano tuition began with Edna Jones, of Walters Road and then Margaret Hughes, of Stepney Place before she became a pupil of D James Bevan of Old Road, gaining, under his tuition, her ALCM and LLCM. Later she received organ lessons with Mr D J Evans in All Saints.

Mattie, a Sunday School teacher at St Alban's Church for 26 years was also chairman of its Ladies' Christian Fellowship for nearly 40 years and a church organist for more than half a century. She often played at St David's Cathedral as well as giving many organ recitals and her talents could often be heard at weddings and funerals. Mattie worked with her husband Les in St Alban's for more than 40 years until she retired in 1998. When he retired as choirmaster before her, one of her organ pupils — Beryl Bailey — took over and the pair enjoyed an equally harmonious musical relationship.

The achievements of Mattie and Les spanned many decades and touched many people. During the war years between 1939 and 1945 the couple formed a concert party and helped raise £1,000 for the town's Spitfire Fund. In that same concert party were Doris Owen, Vera Tiley-James, Anne Anthony and Luther Rees.

For many years St Alban's Church performed sacred cantatas on Good Fridays with Les conducting and Mattie at the organ. Les also wrote many of the pageants which the church performed.

The church choir was affiliated to the Royal School of Church Music and Mattie and Les were chosen to represent South West Wales before the Queen Mother at Addington

Mattie Bateman-Morris outside St Alban's Church and, inset, at its organ.

Palace, Croydon. In 1982 the couple were also invited to a garden party at Buckingham Palace where they met the Queen, the Duke of Edinburgh, the Prince of Wales and also the Princess Royal.

The St Alban's choir holds the United Kingdom record for broadcasting eight times on BBC Radio's Sunday Half Hour programme — each time with Mattie at the organ after which she received many letters of congratulation for her beautiful playing. She was also accompanist to singing star Ivor Emmanuel at Theatre Elli, and accompanied world-famous soprano Gwen Catley and the well-known tenor Gerald Davies in a concert at Zion Chapel. In between all of this Mattie even found time to appear on HTV's Mr and Mrs quiz programme with host Alan Taylor. Together with eldest son Peter she also appeared with Larry Grayson on BBC TV's Generation Game.

I first met Mattie in 1950. A close school pal, David George, had often joked to me: "When I get married you must play the organ at my wedding and when I die you must play at my funeral — Mattie will be quite willing to let you share in the music." Tragically, David died at the age of 14, and his elder brother John George and cousin Keri Gouldstone — later the Rt. Rev. Keri Gouldstone, former Dean of St Asaph — remembered David's words and approached Mattie. Without hesitation she agreed for me to play the closing hymn in the memorial service at St Alban's the Sunday after the funeral. I shall never forget that evening. The final hymn was There's a Friend for Little Children and I was to play it, but Mattie was going to come back to play the Vesper. I was very slim at the time and pulled the organ seat close to the organ. Mattie on the other hand was rather plump, and could not get in to play the Vesper, and she could not budge me nor the seat. The final result was that Mattie played the Vesper by reaching over me from the side of the organ, and I tackled the bass on its pedals. From that night on she and I became friends, and have remained so ever since.

Everyone knew when Mattie was about, her infectious laugh, beaming face and smile with kindness and goodwill were unmistakable. The first Christmas after my mother died she invited me to tea and supper on Christmas Day, a gesture I will never forget.

Everyone in Llanelli Young Music Lovers' Association had a soft spot for Mattie Bateman-Morris who was one of its longest serving vice-presidents until her death in 2005. She played the organ in our grand concerts, conducted and read a lesson in some of our carol festivals, took the chair in one of our concerts, and was a willing participant in very many parlour games. Memorable highlights include Mattie dancing the Can-Can with Dai Smith, John Rees and Gareth Humphreys and singing Daddy Wouldn't Buy Me a Bow Wow and It Ain't Gonna Rain No More, for as well as being a serious musician and an organist who thrilled everybody when they heard her play Mattie, awarded the MBE in 1994, had the ability to be a real comedy performer.

William Roache, better known to millions as Ken Barlow of TV's Coronation Street.

Street Star

William Roache

For more than 45 years William Roache has been a part of the lives and living rooms of millions across the land as Ken Barlow, now the longest surviving member of the characters that appeared in the very first episode of Coronation Street in 1960.

As such he is a character who needs little introduction, but what many may not know is that Derbyshire-born Bill served with the Royal Welsh Fusiliers. I first met him more than 25 years ago in December 1980 when he visited Llanelli as a special guest of the town's Young Music Lovers' Association at its annual Christmas carol festival in Capel Newydd. His unassuming nature was quickly demonstrated. His first words to me were: "Call me Bill."

He had travelled down from Manchester by car and arrived at Capel Newydd at about 6pm, just an hour before the start of the carol festival. Gwennie Lloyd and Mrs May Richards from Capel Newydd had prepared some sandwiches, cakes and a refreshing cuppa for both of us.

Bill made himself quite at home and was soon chatting in a very homely manner, as if he had known us for years.

Later, at the carol festival he commented that the kindness and charm of both Mrs Lloyd and Mrs Richards were typical examples of a real Welsh welcome, before going on to read passages from A Christmas Carol by Charles Dickens and A Child's Christmas At Home by Dylan Thomas in a most delightful manner. He also joined in the community carols with great gusto.

After the festival, Bill, myself and my mother, Blod, were invited to the home of Mr and Mrs John Protheroe in Five Roads for a meal beautifully prepared by Mrs Nans Protheroe, a vice-president of the association. At the time Bill was concerned for his wife Sara, who was ill and his first request to Mrs Protheroe was for permission to phone his wife to enquire about her condition, a gesture typical of the personality of this lovely gentleman.

My mother and Bill got on very well and when we left for home he kissed Mam. With a smile, she immediately informed him that she wouldn't wash her face for a month!

Triniti Presbyterian Chapel, Llanelli in the early 1920s and, inset, one of the greatest preachers to hold the ministry there, Rev. TC Lewis. He served its congregation for 11 years, from 1936 - 1947.

Preaching Power
Rev. TC Lewis

The Rev. TC Lewis was one of Wales's greatest preachers and as the minister of Triniti Presbyterian Chapel, Llanelli, for 11 years from 1936-1947 had an immense influence on my life. My family on both sides were full of admiration and respect for both TC and his marvellous wife Jane.

Rev. Thomas Cyfelach Lewis was, as his middle name clearly hints, a native of Llangyfelach and affectionately known to hundreds throughout Wales as simply TC. He started life as a tinplate worker, but later followed a divinity course at Trefecca College. His first pastorate was at Seion, Seven Sisters, in the Dulais Valley, near Neath, before periods in Llwynbrwydrau, Llansamlet, Tabernacl, Aberaeron, and finally to Triniti, Llanelli. He was given the unique honour to be chosen to give the Davies Lecture at the General Assembly of the Presbyterian Church of Wales in Cardiff in 1944. The subject was Swn y Storm — The Sound of the Storm — a biography of the Welsh poet and hymn writer Islwyn. It was a brilliant lecture, and many thought he should publish it, but unassuming TC resisted. Some of his sermons were masterpieces. When my uncle, Alderman John Griffiths, became Mayor of Llanelli in 1947, the civic service was held in Triniti, and the text on that morning was from the Book of Isaiah: "For unto us a child is born, unto us a Son is given and the government shall be upon his shoulder and his name shall be called Wonderful, Counsellor, Almighty God, the Everlasting Father, The Prince of Peace." Rev. Lewis placed particular emphasis on the word counsellor. It was an unforgettable service, and the civic and military dignitaries present were really touched.

Earlier, Triniti had become the first chapel in Wales to broadcast a morning service on the BBC Home Service in February, 1942. TC's outstanding sermon on that occasion was heard all over the world, not least by Llanelli men WR Howells in the desert in Egypt, and James Herbert serving in Naples, Italy. But many others also listened intently and Rev. Lewis received hundreds of letters from all over the world. His text was from the Book of Genesis where Joseph instructs his brothers to go back to fetch their father Jacob and tells them: "Don't argue on the way home." At the time there was famine in Canaan, and wartime food rationing in Britain. His theme was based on this. "You should not argue on the way because you have: 1, Food; 2, You are brothers and 3, You are going home. He was also a wonderful off-the-cuff speaker, and a unique leader in our weekly fellowship meetings. He would also persuade and encourage others to take part. He could be serious, and once remarked: "Go at people's feet, but don't go under their feet — be humble but don't be trodden on." But TC also had a great sense of humour and loved to tease. One Thursday evening, chapel caretaker, Jenny Thomas, was standing at the door of the vestry. It was a very wet and windy night and that afternoon Jenny had been scrubbing its floor with her usual thoroughness. She was watching people coming in to ensure that they would wipe their feet on the mat, so as not to dirty the vestry floor. Rev. Lewis came in, and she told him to wipe his feet on the mat, because they were dirty, to which he replied: "My feet are clean Jenny fach. I had a bath before I came out. It is my shoes that are dirty." On another occasion one of the elders, Arthur Herbert, and a group of members were gathered outside the chapel, discussing the sermon and services. Arthur saw Rev. Lewis approaching and decided to tease him with the question: "Mr Lewis, do you believe in the devil as a person?" Rev. Lewis was quick on the ball and replied: "Of course I do, I'm speaking to him now."

Additionally, TC loved children, and his monthly children's services were a treat. He was a good poet, and wrote a few pretty pieces of poetry for the younger members of his flock including Y Lili — The Lily — and Y Rhosyn — The Rose. A public speaker and a former school teacher, Mrs Lewis, meanwhile, immersed herself in the life of the chapel and worked with children in the vestry and went out on a missionary basis encouraging children — and adults — into the chapel. Like TC, she was also very well-loved and respected. It was a great blow for TC when she died suddenly in 1945. He never fully regained his confidence and enthusiasm, and retired from being the minister of Triniti in 1947. Nevertheless, he continued to preach with great zeal and fervour keeping in touch with Triniti Chapel until his death in 1953.

He was also one of two preachers in my cousin's induction service at Aberporth in 1949. Sharing the pulpit with him on that occasion was another great preacher, Rev. MP Morgan, of Blaenanerch. Everyone thought Rev. Lewis would never be able to match the preaching of the Rev. Morgan, but it was not to be. In his sermon, Rev. Morgan had spoken of the honour he had been given — a garden party with King George VI at Buckingham Palace. When the time came for TC to preach, his response was that the Rev. Morgan had been given the honour to preach first because he, TC, had not met King George VI. "I haven't been given that honour," said TC, "But I can tell you something about the King of Kings — the Lord Jesus Christ." From there he rose and rose, giving a brilliant sermon that not only matched Rev. Morgan, but surpassed him.

It was an honour for me to know and learn from this wonderful gentleman from the earliest of times when he would visit our Hick Street home and I would, ask him: "Would you like a game of bagatelle?" He never refused. When we had finished he would always shake my hand and squeeze it tightly. I couldn't release my hand from his firm grip. I shall never forget the Rev. TC Lewis nor indeed his later gift to me. It was his personal Old Notation Hymn Book. Today that book with its hand-written Welsh inscription — Rhodd i Gethin – oddiwrth TC Lewis, 1948 — remains one of my most treasured possessions.

Three of a Kind
Vera, Elsie and Awen

Three well-known characters who in different ways contributed greatly to the cultural life of Llanelli were Vera Tiley-James, Elsie Jones and Awen Marsh-Jenkins.

Vera Tiley-James was the eldest of three children who was a life-long member of Siloah Congregational Chapel, where she was the choirmistress for a period. Her contribution as a contralto soloist in Llanelli was immeasurable and spanned nearly 60 years of charity work. Although ill-health stopped Vera from singing in public in later years, music and song remained close to her heart.

Vera married Cyril James and became known throughout the town as Madam Vera Tiley-James, her rich contralto voice giving much pleasure down the years. Her mother Mrs Gertie Tiley was also a very good soprano soloist, and a member of John Thomas's famous Llanelli Royal Choral Society which sang at Windsor Castle for King Edward VII, Queen Alexandra and The Kaiser of Germany in 1912. Vera, her mother and two aunts — Martha and Edith — were fundamental members of Robert Charles's Cymric Glee Singers. Vera was the contralto soloist with the choir for 21 years until it disbanded in 1956. This choir entertained audiences all over Wales, giving hundreds of concerts. For 23 years, Vera was also a very active member of my concert party, and sang with me at the piano in more than 400 concerts.

Among our memorable moments performing together was when she sang the role of the gipsy Azucena in highlights of Verdi's Il Trovatore — a part she sang with huge success at the Public Hall in Llanelli Market, as was her performance in the Sound of Music four years later. Another highlight was in 1967, again in the Public Hall, when she and her mother took lead parts and also made most of the costumes for the musical Holiday In Holland — no mean achievement with a cast of 90.

Often mother and daughter sang duets and both performed on one occasion in a concert at St David's Cathedral with myself at the organ. Vera, who died in 2003, also sang in many concerts with such famous names as Richie Thomas, the well-known Welsh tenor; opera star Rita Hunter, Trixie Walters and twice with the Morriston Orpheus Choir. Her most memorable solos were Craig yr Oesoedd, He Was Despised, from the Messiah; I Have Lost My Euridyce from Gluck's opera Orpheus; My Hero and Curly Headed Babi.

Well known Llanelli musician Frank Phillips, music teacher at the Boys' Grammar School, once remarked that: "Vera Tiley-James has the best diction I have ever heard

Vera Tiley-James, Elsie Jones and Awen Marsh as they were pictured when featured in my Solo Note column in the Llanelli Star. It was taken while they were on holiday together.

from a singer. Every word is crystal clear." What a compliment to an outstanding lady whose rich contralto voice gave so much pleasure to the people of Llanelli.

Awen Marsh was born and bred in Capel Als, and won first prize in the 12-16 piano solo at the Royal National Eisteddfod of Wales in Fishguard in 1936. It was the same year as two other Llanelli girls won first prizes there. Megan Griffiths, also of Capel Als, took the recitation 12-16 prize and Betty Davies, of Zion Chapel, first prize for the soprano solo. What a year that was for the town, because Llanelli Choral Society conducted by Edgar Thomas, with Madam Florence Holloway as accompanist, also won first prize. Later, Awen gained the diplomas of LRAM and ARCM as a pianist, and then married David Jenkins of Emma Street.

Awen Marsh-Jenkins was the organist of Dock Chapel for 25 years before returning to her native Capel Als as deputy organist until she died in 1977, aged 57. She was accompanist to the Cymric Glee Singers, under the baton of Robert Charles, for 21 years, hence her link with Vera Tiley-James.

Awen taught for a brief period in Llanelli Girls' Grammar School where she forged a link with Elsie Jones. She had many piano pupils and successes in examinations and Eisteddfodau, taught music with me jointly in Loughor Youth Club and was also accompanist to Llanelli Choral Society for over 20 years. During this period the society took part in a concert with the London Symphony Orchestra conducted by Sir Adrian Boult, in the former Regal cinema. In a piano rehearsal a few days before the concert Sir Adrian publicly praised Awen's excellent and polished accompaniment.

After Awen's death her husband David presented me with her personal hymn book and wrote on it: "To Gethin, in memory of Awen — David." It remains a treasured possession. When David died, his sister Nancy from Emma Street also presented me with two 78rpm records that Awen had made in the years after she won at the National Eisteddfod. They too are still treasured possessions.

Elsie Jones was another of Llanelli's talented musical jewels. Small in stature, she possessed a bubbly personality and a big heart. A graduate of the University of Wales, she taught music for more than 20 years at Coleshill Girls' School, and ended her career with 15 years as a Welsh teacher at Llanelli Girls' Grammar School. Fluent in both Welsh and English, Elsie was an orator who could leave her audience spellbound, whether in school in front of a class of pupils or before an adult audience. She loved teaching and was in her element with young people.

For years she worked for the Urdd and the Llanelli Aelwyd, with Olwen Williams, Myfanwy Davies and Loti Rees-Hughes. A life-long member of Bethel Baptist Chapel, she toiled faithfully over the years. Her Nativity plays and pageants were superb and her carol festivals in Coleshill school a town treat. She was a founder vice-president of the Llanelli Young Music Lovers' Association, and worked diligently with the young people until her death in 1978 at the age of 74.

In 1967, Elsie jointly produced with Dai Smith, deputy headmaster of Llanelli Boys' Grammar School, Pasiant Genedigaeth Iesu Grist, which had been especially written for my concert party and friends by Meiriona J Rees, of Triniti Chapel.

On one occasion I accompanied Elsie to the Grand Theatre, Swansea, to see international opera star Pauline Tinsley sing the role of Abigail in the Welsh National Opera's production of Nabucco. We had a meal with Pauline beforehand, and she asked us backstage after the performance. She then invited Elsie to sit on Nabucco's throne. Later in the week Pauline told me on the telephone: "That little Miss Jones is a dynamic personality, she has even persuaded me to learn Welsh — the language of Heaven."

Anne Ziegler and Webster Booth — they sang several times for the Royal family.

Signature Sounds
Anne Ziegler and Webster Booth

Without a doubt, one of the most famous signature tunes of the last century was Only a Rose from the musical Vagabond King. It is a tune that became synonymous with the legendary husband and wife duo of Anne Ziegler and Webster Booth. It became their signature tune after their resounding success in the London production of the popular show in 1942.

Anne met Webster towards the end of 1937 when they starred in a film version of the opera Faust. A year later on November 5, 1938, they became husband and wife and remained happily married for 45 years until Webster's death in 1983. Anne told me once how she remembered driving on their honeymoon night with Guy Fawkes bonfires blazing and fireworks exploding all around them. For a quarter of a century, the couple remained top of the bill performers. They were household names throughout Britain becoming involved with films, radio, music hall and television— true super stars of their time. Their blend and harmonies pleased and soothed many thousands throughout the war years in particular. They took part in the 1941 London Palladium production of Gangway and in 1944 they performed in the longest run of any Variety Bill at the Palladium, with Bebe Daniels, Ben Lyon the famous xylophone player; Teddy Brown and comedian Max Miller. The same year they appeared in a film entitled Waltz Time with George Robey, Richard Tauber and Albert Sandler.

On their seventh wedding anniversary in 1945 they had the honour of appearing in a Royal Command Performance show. They sang several times for the Royal family in Buckingham Palace and Windsor and in February 1948, they were invited to sing on a Sunday morning for King George V1 and the Queen Mother at the private chapel of the Royal Lodge, Windsor. After the service they shared refreshments with their Royal hosts. While Webster is regarded as one of the greatest oratorio tenors ever, his lyrical voice was seen a great advantage in opera as well, Anne was an expert in lighter music and particularly so as principal boy in pantomimes. For years she was in great demand in these fields while Webster continued his oratorio work.

Anne told me that her greatest ambition was to sing the soprano part in Handel's Messiah. This was achieved, when she sang with Webster, the Huddersfield Choral Society and Liverpool Philharmonic Orchestra under the baton of Sir Malcolm Sargent, in Blackpool in 1948. Later the couple toured Australia, New Zealand and South Africa where they lived for nearly 25 years before returning to live in Llandudno in 1976 because both loved Wales, its people and the language. I first saw Anne and Webster performing with pianist Semprini when I was a young boy on holiday with my parents in Llandudno and then again in 1951 at a Sunday concert with famous piano duetists Rawicz and Landauer. The following year, Anne Ziegler and Webster Booth were sharing top billing for a week of variety at the Pier Pavilion, Llandudno, with Gert and Daisy — sisters Elsie and Doris Waters.

At the height of her career Anne Ziegler's gowns were made by Norman Hartnell the Queen's dressmaker and were fabulous creations, enhanced by her own magical artistry and command of the stage. I recall my mother saying: "I wonder what Anne Ziegler will be wearing tonight." On that occasion she was not disappointed as the star stepped onto the stage in a black crinoline dress with sprays of pink roses adorning it and on another occasion it was an equally impressive dress with cape of scarlet taffeta. After their return from South Africa Anne Ziegler designed and made her own evening dresses showing what a great needle-woman she was as well as a superb singer and actress.

My first meeting with the gifted and talented couple was when they came to Llanelli in November 1979 to sing for Llanelli Young Music Lovers' Association at Lloyd Street Chapel. They did a 30-minute spot of about eight duets and Anne also sang a solo. Paul Williams introduced them and I was privileged to play for them.

A year and a half later, they were singing in Old Tyme Music Hall at the Patti Pavilion, Swansea and requested that I accompany them. Anne who is an excellent pianist herself, insisted that the grand piano was placed on the stage so that I would be on the same level as them. What a thrill it was for me to accompany this legendary couple. As I played Only a Rose when they entered from different sides of the stage the packed audience applauded loudly. Webster asked me if, when they sang The Keys of Heaven, I would get up from the piano stool and say: "Let me have a go Webster." and he in reply would say: "Sit down and go back to the piano." Of course I was only too happy to join in the proceedings in this way, particularly in the finale which involved me walking down the stage between them. It was great fun and a great honour to boot. Afterwards we were all invited by the Lord Mayor of Swansea to his parlour for a reception, photographs and signing of the city's guest register. What a wonderful evening it was.

Sadly Webster Booth died in 1984, but Anne and I remained in contact until her death at the age of 93 in 2003. She gave me copies of two of Webster's tenor solos with his name on in his own handwriting as a memento which remain in my musical treasury. On one occasion when I was a guest at her home in Penrhyn Beach, Llandudno, my mother was very ill and Anne kindly made a special tape recording of Drink To Me Only especially for her. One of our concert party trips to Llandudno in 1991 was also graced with her presence for lunch. This was repeated when 40 pupils from Ysgol y Strade visited the town accompanied by teachers Mavis Williams, Helen Lane, Iwan Rees and myself. The pupils were delighted to meet her and she signed autographs for many of them.

Civic Salute
Uncle John and Auntie Gertie

My uncle John Griffiths was one of the most popular mayors of Llanelli — and his wife Gertie, one of the town's most popular mayoresses. They were both from the Machynys area and their civic year ran from 1946 through to 1947.

Auntie Gertie's family were faithful members of Dock Chapel, and I remember her telling me how much she enjoyed the playing of Dick Prosser the organist there. When she married John Griffiths, she became a member of Triniti Presbyterian Chapel, where he was an elder and Sunday School teacher. Uncle John became a borough councillor in 1939 and in 1942 he and Auntie Gertie became Deputy Mayor and Mayoress to Councillor and Mrs Harry Bowen. In 1946, they themselves became the town's first citizens and proved to be one of the most popular civic partnerships of the time.

For many years the mayor and mayoress had driven to their civic service in the official car in the Mayoral procession, but Gertie insisted that she and John walk all the way from the Town Hall in the procession to Triniti Chapel, New Dock Road, and afterwards walk all the way back again. This was indeed a brave decision as she was a stout lady, but her gesture won the hearts of the hundreds who lined the route. She looked very regal and stately. Throughout the war years she had already won great respect in Llanelli for her marvellous work with the WVS.

Another gesture that won them much public applause came as a result of the fact that although Uncle John was a member of the Labour Party, he would not always toe the line, sometimes opposing his fellow Labour colleagues. For example he supported Independent councillor Ted Howells's adoption as mayor, instead of helping to put a Labour mayor in, saying it was the person who was important not the party.

On one occasion he quarrelled with both Alderman W Douglas Hughes and his wife, Alderman Loti Rees-Hughes when all three were governors of the grammar school. My uncle was their chairman. He gave the casting vote for Mr Stanley G Rees to be made the new headmaster in succession to Mr TV Shaw. Loti and Douglas wanted another candidate — connected with the Labour Party — to be headmaster.

Four years later when the Duke of Edinburgh opened the new grammar school in Pwll and praised the eventual headmaster Mr Stanley Rees, saying that he was one of the best headmasters he had ever met, Loti and Douglas made their peace with Uncle John when she said: "John Griffiths you were right and we were wrong." From that day on uncle

John and Alderman Douglas Hughes and his wife Loti became very good friends. In 1958 Uncle John received one of the greatest honours that could be accorded to anyone when he became the subject of BBC TV's This is your Life programme with Eamon Andrews.

In those days it was rare for lay or ordinary people to be chosen. Usually famous film and TV personalities or national politicians were the only ones whose lives were spotlighted at that time. It turned on Uncle John for his public speaking and oratory skills. I remember the night well. It was November and Uncle John thought he was going to speak on BBC Radio Wales so he was going to catch the 3pm train up to the studios. His daughter Betty had asked my mother Blod to see that uncle John caught the train. She was not to show him she was also in the station so she hid around a corner.

Auntie Gertie was in ill health and could not take part in the programme, so my mother and I together with two other aunts had to go to prepare the way to let her know that her husband would be on television. What a celebration we all had in Westbury Street that night.

Taking part in the programme were his daughter Betty, son Geraint, his brother Davie and two chapel friends from Triniti — Dai and Jenny, Ty Capel. In a way Betty followed in the footsteps of her mother becoming Mayoress of Llandovery, twice.

Uncle John and Auntie Gertie opened their home to many visitors — ministers, concert artists, in fact everyone received a royal welcome at their Westbury Street home. John was a master at making home-made wines — rhubarb, parsnip, parsley, elderberry, beetroot and potato, and once when he threw the dregs out onto waste ground a cockerel ate them, and became drunk. He was also a member of my concert party for 14 years, and with his comedy items he gave hours of pleasure and enjoyment to hundreds of people.

On one occasion he appeared with the concert party in a musical at the parish hall. The musical was Ahoy There and in the last act he had to wear a full evening suit — tails and bow tie. In an after dinner speech to a Womens' Institute some time later he joked: "When my wife Gertie saw me walk on the stage in evening dress she thought I looked so handsome, her tummy turned over."

He was a very kindly soul believing the best about everybody and had a wonderful sense of humour even in church and chapel matters. After his death many pensioners paid tribute to his generosity. Many a widow had a 10 shilling note as a Christmas box, he paid bus fares for pensioners and exhibited many other kindnesses.

John and Gertie Griffiths — Llanelli's first citizens as Mayor and Mayoress, 1946-47.

Gethin Hughes shares a moment with Harriet Lewis, better known to many as Maggie'r Post of S4C TV's popular Pobl Y Cwm soap opera.

Stitches and Stamps

Harriet Lewis

When Harriet Lewis arrived at Ysgol y Strade canteen one Saturday evening in May 1979, for the annual dinner of the Llanelli Young Music Lover's Association, she electrified the place. Small in stature, but large and dynamic in personality — that was Harriet. On that occasion she was one of the special guests, the others being Madam Lynne Richards, Tycroes, and Rev. Elfed ap Nefydd Roberts, principal of the Theological College at Aberystwyth.

When Harriet rose to address us, we were all aware that one of Wales's best-loved personalities was taking the stage and believe me she did it in style. We were kept in stitches for 15 solid minutes and ached with laughter and enjoyment. Some of the stories she narrated were acted out in front of us, tales like the schoolboy who informed her that his mother was in hospital having her 'ballbearings' removed. What he meant to say of course was gallstones!

Known to thousands as Maggie'r Post in the popular soap-opera Pobl Y Cwm, Harriet was born in Trebanos, in the Swansea Valley where she was a faithful member of Goshen Congregational Chapel, and began working full time for the BBC in Wales after retiring from a career in teaching. She had worked part-time for them, mainly on Radio Wales and Radio Cymru for many years before.

She was in Welsh programmes such as Awr y Plant, Sut Hwyl, Peidiwch a Son, Raligamps, and Teulu Siop y Gornel working with such people as Rachel Thomas, Olive Michael, Ennis Tinnuche, Gwenyth Petty, Prysor Williams and the late Dilys Davies from Swansea. Two of her famous catchphrases were: "Watch aur neu clin bren" which means "a Gold watch or a wooden leg" from Raligamps and "S'dim bricsyn bach o siwgr gyda chi hyd 'fori" or "Can you lend me a little sugar until tomorrow?" After being asked if what she was given was enough for her, she would reply in Welsh "Enough for a week — I'll be back again before long though to beg another favour."

She worked on Raligamps with George David, Esme Lewis, Ifor Rees and Dafydd Evans. Harriet was a regular participant in Welsh Rarebit, which was produced by the well known Mai Jones. During that programme she could be heard during The Adventures of Tommy Trouble, with Gunstone Jones and Eynon Evans.

After her great success in the Young Music Lovers' Association dinner, Harriet and I became friends, and she began taking the pulpit at Triniti Chapel. In that role she was a

Sir Geraint Evans and his wife Lady Brenda Evans in a dressing room meeting with Gethin Hughes at Covent Garden.

completely different person taking her work seriously and with reverence and respect. She led the Sunday Services in Triniti on many occasions and members thoroughly enjoyed the experience. On one occasion a coachload of us went to see Harriet and Rachel Thomas at the Grand Theatre, Swansea, in the play Arsenic and Old Lace. Afterwards we all had great fun in her dressing room. Later, friends gave me a birthday dinner in Pontlliw and as a special surprise Harriet, who died in November 1999, had agreed to attend.

Knight of Knights
Sir Geraint Evans

Sir Geraint Evans was known the world over not only as one of the greatest opera singers in the world, but also as a genial, well-loved, dynamic, Welsh-speaking personality. Proof of his unbridled love for Wales and the Welsh language is that he bought a house in Aberaeron in which to spend his well-earned retirement. He settled with great ease into the community and was well-liked by the locals.

His love for the sea and fishing was well-known and he enjoyed trips on his boat out into Cardigan Bay. I can visualise Sir Geraint on his boat now, singing the famous baritone solo by RS Hughes: Y Dymestl — The Tempest. His performance of this Welsh masterpiece was well-known throughout the musical world and when his rich baritone voice combined with action and facial expression, one could not fail to see the raging sea and the boats on it being tossed from wave to wave.

Sir Geraint was an expert on Handel arias and his performance of the famous bass solos from Messiah was spine-chilling and thrilling, but this outstanding Welsh baritone will always be remembered as a giant of the operatic stage. His annual visits to Covent Garden, London; Metropolitan Opera, New York; La Scala, Milan; San Francisco Opera and Vienna State Opera, places where he gave outstanding and brilliant performances of Falstaff, Don Pasquale, Dr. Dulcamara, Leperello, Figaro, Don Basillio and many more, were highlights of the operatic calendar. Well-loved by fellow top-liners like Pavarotti, Domingo, Carreras, Joan Sutherland, Maria Callas and Boris Christoff, this Knight of knights was someone Wales can be more proud of than ever, even to this day.

A year before Sir Geraint retired from the operatic stage, I organised a coach trip to London for the weekend to see him perform in Covent Garden. We witnessed an unforgettable performance of the comedy Don Pasquale. Sir Geraint took the title role, with Loughor tenor Ryland Davies, Australian bass Jonathan Summers and the then young Italian soprano Luciana Serra the other parts.

Madam Peggy Williams of Trimsaran, knew we were going and had phoned her sister, Anita, a neighbour of Sir Geraint, to say we were coming. We were staying at the Mount Royal Hotel and as we sat at our table eating our evening meal, the head waiter came and informed me that I was wanted on the telephone. It was Peggy's sister telling me that Sir Geraint was overjoyed we were in London and would love to talk to us after the performance. We were told to stay in our seats until the other 2,000 people had left the theatre before making our way to the crush bar in the Royal Circle. The following night after a first class performance of Don Pasquale, we did as we were told and made our way to the allotted area. When we arrived we were very surprised indeed. There to greet us were 10 small tables each seating four people and laden with ham, cheese and tomato sandwiches along with bottles of wine. We were told by the theatre ushers to sit at the tables and help ourselves and that Sir Geraint would join us later.

About half an hour later Sir Geraint arrived, immaculately dressed in blue blazer, grey trousers, white shirt and tie, accompanied by Lady Evans, his brother and sister-in-law; his son and daughter-in-law; Lord and Lady Hooson; Ryland Davies and Jonathan Summers.

Earlier in the day on the suggestion of Edwina Barney, one of our party, I bought a box of chocolates as a gift for Lady Evans just in case we met her. I thanked Sir Geraint for his welcome and kindness and offered him the chocolates for Lady Evans who was at the other end of the crush bar. His response was to shout with delight across the theatre: "Come quick, Brenda, they've brought you some chocolates from Llanelli." He then suggested that he, Ryland Davies and Jonathan Summers would stand behind the bar, while we stood on the other side to speak to them and have autographs.

One of our party, Margaret Skinner, explained to Sir Geraint that my mother and Margaret Edwards were semi-invalids and would not be able to walk and stand by the bar. He assured her that the two ladies would not be overlooked, and, after finishing signing autographs for the rest of the party, the three singers moved to the table where my mother and Mrs Edwards were seated, and sat and spoke with them for about 10 minutes. Finally the three performers kissed the ladies and that ended a marvellous experience — a night of nights with a knight of knights.

A year later I had the privilege of meeting Sir Geraint again when, with Iwan Rees, I visited the Royal Opera House, Covent Garden, to hear him sing his final operatic performance — Dr Dulcamara in L'Elisir D'amore by Donizetti.

He invited both of us to his dressing room after the performance for a chat with Lady Evans and himself, and to take photographs and see the costumes that he wore for the performance. While we were in the dressing room a group of Italian musicians came to talk to Sir Geraint while Iwan and I spoke with Lady Evans. As we were chatting, Lady Evans became aware that Sir Geraint had his hands on their shoulders and arms and she said: "I wish Geraint wouldn't paw people so much. We, the Welsh are so demonstrative and emotional and some foreigners can be very touchy about being pawed." What a wonderful partnership and a lovely happy marriage — the tenderness of Lady Evans for the great man. Sir Geraint was indeed an operatic giant.

Welcome Visits
Lady Olwen Carey Evans

For five years Lady Olwen Carey Evans was a Patron of Llanelli Young Music Lovers' Association and that is when we struck up a firm friendship that was to be maintained throughout the rest of her life.

Olwen Lloyd George was the middle child of five born to the late David Lloyd George — former Prime Minister and Chancellor of the Exchequer — and his wife Margaret. Her elder brother and sister were Richard and Mair and her younger brother and sister were Gwilym and Megan. This sprightly lady who lived at Eisteddfa, Criccieth, the home of her husband Harley Street specialist Sir Tom Carey Evans, who she married in 1917, was the last surviving member of the Lloyd George family. Lady Olwen's husband was a cousin of Lord Snowdon former husband of Princess Margaret and Eisteddfa was the family home of the Armstrong-Jones family.

I was welcomed there on many occasions by Lady Olwen and every time I visited her with different friends, she gave the same royal Welsh welcome — entertaining us with tea, bara brith, Welsh cakes and scones. Even though she lived in a mansion and enjoyed a grand lifestyle she had always prepared this feast herself, wheeled it in on a trolley and served it too — even when she was 94.

My first visit was with Gareth Wyn Thomas who at the time was vice-chairman of the Music Lovers' Association and then I revisited Lady Olwen when the Urdd Eisteddfod was held in Pwllheli in 1982. I had mentioned to her on the telephone that I was taking a party of schoolchildren from Ysgol y Strade to compete there. She immediately invited me to call and said: "Bring your friends." Three of the staff accompanied me, leaving another four to look after the children.

Among those who accompanied me were teachers Susan Tiplady, Mavis Williams and local historian John Edwards, who was then head of the history department at the school. He was fascinated with this remarkable character, who had prepared refreshments for the four of us and squash and sandwiches for 45 children — she had expected the entire coachload of children to visit her that day. What a kind hearted lady.

Susan, Mavis, John and myself thoroughly enjoyed our afternoon and it was he who persuaded her to write her autobiography which was published two years later, when she was 92. She said she wanted to put right what she described as some untruths stated in an earlier, much-watched, TV series about her famous father.

Chatting with Lady Olwen Carey Evans in the delightful garden of her Snowdonia home.

My next visit was some years later with another friend from Ysgol y Strade, Iwan Rees, head of the economics department and former captain of Llanelli Wanderers rugby team. This time Lady Olwen was lighting a fire, but still insisted we stay for tea. The first thing she told Iwan and myself was: "Tell your friend John Edwards that he influenced me to write my autobiography." She continued to inform Iwan, that when she went to draw her pension every week she said: "Diolch Tada" — Thank you father. It was of course Lloyd George who established the old age pension system.

My last visit was with Garry Nicholas another Ysgol y Strade figurehead and S4C personality. It was when she was 94 and still driving. At that time my mother was very ill and she recorded a taped message with Garry asking her some questions. Lady Olwen had recently been to a special dinner party at No 10 Downing Street given by the then Prime Minister, Margaret Thatcher and attended by the Queen and Duke of Edinburgh. Among those there with her were former Prime Ministers, Edward Heath, Harold Wilson, Alec Douglas-Home, James Callaghan and Harold Macmillan, The Lord Chancellor, Viscount Hailsham and the Archbishop of Canterbury as well as children of former prime ministers, Mary Churchill and Sheila Lockhead — Ramsey McDonald's daughter. Lady Olwen commented to us: "The Queen and her husband were very nice as was poor old Macmillan. He was very frail, but he is 90."

Amazingly dear Lady Olwen was herself 94. At 95 she was still driving her car and worshipping at her chapel three times on Sundays. Until she died at the age of 98, she was one of the few women who could be addressed as Lady Olwen Carey Evans or Dame Olwen Carey Evans in her own right. But whatever she was addressed as, she was still a down-to-earth ordinary Welsh girl — a true daughter who really could say: "Lloyd George was my father."

Triniti Team
Tom and Mary Etta

The names of Mr and Mrs Tom Jones were well known in musical circles throughout South Wales mainly because Tom and his wife Mary Etta were in charge of singing in Triniti Chapel, Llanelli, for decades. Tom became choirmaster there in 1900 and remained so until his death 58 years later in 1958. As if this was not enough of a record, his wife surpassed this.

Mary Etta Hughes became organist at Triniti in 1898 and worked with my grandfather, David Hughes, for two years until Tom took over in 1900. Mary Etta holds the record in Wales having been organist for 71 years — 26 of those on the harmonium and 45 on the pipe organ. She started as organist at the tender age of 11 and incredibly didn't retire from the role until she was 82.

In 1922 she married Tom Jones at Triniti, and so began one of the best known husband and wife partnerships in South Wales. The couple were often called upon to conduct and play in Gymanfa Ganu — Welsh singing festivals — all over South Wales. Mary Etta also played for Robert Charles at Capel Newydd when the choir performed oratorios or cantatas.

Mary Etta and Tom were noted for their interpretation of Welsh hymns and people travelled for many miles to hear the Triniti choir sing choruses such as Worthy Is The Lamb, the Hallelujah Chorus from Handel's Messiah and The Heaven's Are Telling from Haydn's Creation, as well as Welsh anthems like Teyrnasoedd y Ddaear and Dyn A Aned O Wraig.

No one could read a hymn like Tom Jones. He knew exactly how to interprate the individual messages. Not only was he an excellent musician, but a first class elocutionist teaching pupils to recite as well as sing, and he won many prizes for recitation.
Tom also understood children. For years he was an elder and superintendent of the Sunday School in Triniti often promising them a gold watch or seat by the window on the train for the annual trip to Ferryside if they sang well! One of six children he was born in Russell Street, Llanelli, worked as a coal merchant and later as a Llanelli Borough Council rent collector.

Mary Etta was one of four children and followed her mother Marged behind the counter of a grocery shop in Dillwyn Street. She was an excellent organist and her renderings of Welsh hymns in the Communion service were tear-jerkers. She was not a recital

Tom and Mary Etta Jones — their services were often called upon for gymanfa ganu across South Wales.

organist, but no one could beat her for playing a hymn or for creating atmosphere in a service. She never spoke in public and could not even play an Amen without music, but her contribution to the life of Llanelli was immense. I recall one of her sayings, "Champagne to our real friends — real pain to our sham friends."

Tom and Mary Etta Jones will be remembered as long as Triniti Chapel remains open. So great was their contribution to its success that after their deaths the elders placed a commemorative plaque on the organ — for 58 and 71 years of glorious, dedicated service respectively.

During their lifetime the couple conducted and played in many operettas such as Giant's Castle, Idle Ben and Holiday on the Sands. They also trained hundreds of children in various skills during the long time they were in charge of music in Triniti Chapel.

Winging It
Cissie Killick-Hughes

My first recollection of Cissie Killick-Hughes was in Morfa School Hall in 1943, when she was playing for the Wings for Victory charity concert party. At that time she wore her hair in a bun, and I can see her now at the piano on the stage and playing with gusto the wartime sounds, and in particular "Bless 'em all, bless 'em all, the long and the short and the tall."

Cissie, now in her nineties, from Trostre Road, married Arthur Hughes of Trinity Terrace, in Christ Church, Llanelli, in August 1940, and ever since she has been known to the people of Llanelli as Cissie Killick-Hughes. From 1930-1941 she was the organist of Christ Church, and for seven years was accompanist to the Western Male Voice, under the baton of WE Phillips. She followed Madam Florence Holloway as accompanist to Llanelli Ladies' Choir, conducted by Edgar Thomas.

I remember Cissie in a concert at the old Regal Cinema, she was accompanist to the choir, and Madam Holloway was accompanying the four artists — Isobel Baillie, Mary Jarred, Henry Wendon and Robert Easton. My mother Blod, who had a lovely voice, enjoyed a celebrity concert, and she always took me to the Sunday evening concerts — after attending evening service in Triniti Chapel, of course! On this occasion the talk all around us as we sat in the Regal was of sympathy for Madam Holloway, whose husband Doddie — one of the well-known Holloway's garage family had died. The Holloway family had implored their sister-in-law to continue with the concert, even though it was only two days after the funeral. Cissie and Florence both wore their hair in a bun, and everyone admired Cissie that night for wearing a black frock, identical to Madam Holloway's as a mark of respect.

Cissie was another who taught piano to generations of Llanelli children in her front parlour, and accompanied ballet classes for 30 years. She was also accompanist for Llanelli Choral Society for many years playing under many conductors. They included Idris Griffiths, Wyn Morris, Elwyn Jones, Penri Williams and John Hywel Williams. During the conductorship of the latter she worked with Jean Williams as piano duet with Mattie Bateman-Morris at the organ for a performance of Noah's Flood, at All Saints' Church with Llanelli Choral Society, Hywel Girls Choir, All Saints' Choir and Coleshill Boys' School Choir. During 60 years as an accompanist in Llanelli, she also accompanied such artists as Josephine Barstow, Maureen Guy, John Mitchinson, Raimund Herrinx and Stuart Burrows. I worked with Cissie for three years in Llanelli Amateur Operatic Society.

Cissie Killick Hughes — another of those dedicated stalwarts who taught piano to generations of aspiring Llanelli musicians.

I was the founder conductor and Cissie, along with Sybil Perrott and Beryl Bailey, was a founder accompanist. It was a very happy time for us all — staging The Gondoliers' and The Arcadians — and I will always treasure the partnership I had with Cissie who is now in her mid-nineties.

For many years she has been a faithful and extremely loyal vice-president of Llanelli Young Music Lovers' Association and although ill health prevented her from taking as active a part as she would like, she made an effort to be present as often as is possible. Janet followed in her mother's footsteps, becoming the youngest organist in Wales. For some years Janet was organist of St David's Church, New Dock, Llanelli, from the age of 12 to 18.

String Time
Nancy and Elvet

Nancy Jones and her family from Ropewalk Road, Llanelli, were all faithful members of Dock Chapel. At an early age she learned the violin and played in the chapel orchestra. Many who heard Nancy playing were full of praise and said that she produced a beautiful tone and sound on the instrument. They hinted that one day she would be one of Llanelli's greatest violinists. They were not far wrong for in 1936 Nancy Jones gained her ARCM Teacher's Diploma and started teaching the instrument.

In 1942 Nancy married Elvet Marks and joined her husband as a member of Capel Als. Elvet, who worked in local government, was also an excellent violinist and soon this popular and talented couple had started their equally popular Elvet Marks Orchestra which played in concerts and various other productions all over Wales.

Elvet never taught, but hundreds of youngsters benefited from Nancy's very capable musical skills and she turned out dozens of first class violinists, many of whom became well-known musicians. Nancy was a beautiful solo violinist, and she and Elvet often played violin duets. I joined the Elvet Marks Trio on more than one occasion with tea dances and balls in the Ritz Ballroom — Elvet and Nancy on violin, Tom Hughes on cello, and myself on piano. We had many happy times.

Nancy Marks, could justifiably be called the Queen of Llanelli violinists — a well respected musician and personality. With Iris Williams, another excellent Llanelli violinist, and her sister Gertie they charmed audiences in the town with their skillful, stylish playing. Like Nancy, Iris also taught hundreds of pupils, while sister Gertie made her mark as an accomplished dressmaker.

During the silent film era Nancy played in Llanelli cinemas with D James Bevan and Madam Florence Holloway, who was also an able violinist. She also used to play violin and piano duets with Cissie Killick-Hughes. Elvet was a member of Llanelli County School Orchestra under the direction of Frank Phillips, and for years after Elvet left the County School he and Nancy would go back to help Frank when required.

Elvet and Nancy had a very talented daughter, Anne-Marie, who gained her BA (Music) at Aberystwyth University and is now head of music at Carmarthenshire Sixth Form College's Graig campus. After Elvet's death, Nancy continued with her involvement in the world of music. For me that was particularly fortuitous on one occasaion in 1982.

Nancy and Elvet Marks, who made music almost everywhere they went.

I was musical director of Llanelli Operatic Society and we were performing The Arcadians. At the time I was suffering from 'flu and taking antibiotics which made me feel drowsy and sleepy during the performances. Nancy would watch me like a mother and poke me with her violin bow when the musical numbers came and the orchestra had to play.

The couple will always be remembered for their brilliant performances of oratorios in character form with Capel Als Choral Society and orchestra during productions such as Elijah, Samson and The Messiah. What stood out was the close harmony, understanding and friendship that existed between Dr. Haydn Morris, Elvet and Nancy Marks and Sydney Morgan and this shone through in their performances. When Nancy died a few years ago a great light went out on the Llanelli music scene.

Fairy Godmother
Cynthia Morgan

Cynthia Morgan was a very pretty woman with a gorgeous smile, always immaculately and stylishly dressed. She was brought up in New Road, Dafen, attended Halfway Primary School, as it was known in those days, then Llanelli Girls' Grammar School, before finally gaining her teaching certificate at a domestic science college.

Conveniently for her Cynthia did not have to change her name when she married Hugh Morgan, a grandson of former Mayor of Llanelli, Morgan Morgan, some time before I made her acquaintance when I joined the staff of Ysgol Y Strade. When I started my duties as music teacher there in September 1965 I was immediately made very welcome by Megan Evans, Renee Evans and Cynthia Morgan. The three were inseparable friends and took me — the youngest on the staff — under their wings. Megan Evans taught cookery and Renee Evans physical education.

I knew Cynthia for around 11 years. She was the needlework teacher and the standard of her teaching and her work was first class. Everyone in Ysgol y Strade — pupils and teachers alike — loved and admired this unique person. They thought of her as a fairy princess. She was always the wardrobe mistress for the school productions — Aladdin, Cinderella, Robin Hood, Red Riding Hood, Aladdin in Welsh, Cinderella in Welsh and Stori Handel. We always gave six performances at the school hall to capacity audiences. People would be clamouring for tickets and some would book three months in advance. Without exception every year, one of the highlights would be the costumes created by Cynthia Morgan. They were simply superb.

She was a very understanding and sensitive person, and many pupils took their problems to her, because they were sure of a sympathetic ear and good advice. Cynthia was a loyal and supportive colleague and I soon became big friends with her husband Hugh and their two daughters Beth and Jenny who lived then at Denham Avenue. Every Christmas Cynthia would make me an iced cake with a musical emblem on it and Megan a special fancy sponge. Both these ladies thoroughly spoiled me, particularly on one occasion while I was away from school for three months because of illness.

Cynthia was a very good mixer, and could adapt herself to any company. On one occasion a group of us decided to go in a mini-bus for dinner at The Caswell Bay Hotel. She was the only one of the school staff on the bus, but soon became friends with Ethel Walters, Elsie Jones, Anne Anthony, Betty Tovey, Vera Tiley-James, Meiriona Rees and Margaret Williams — we had a wonderful evening. Cynthia's favourite phrase

Cynthia Morgan — an understanding and sensitive person.

was: No Problem! It was one she used regularly. I remember once when I happened to mention that international opera soprano, Pauline Tinsley was singing the role of Lady Macbeth in the Grand Theatre, Swansea, but because I was a non-driver and times of trains were inconvenient, I would not be able to go. Before the words were out of my mouth Cynthia answered: "No problem. I can take you in my car. I'd love to see Macbeth and hear Pauline Tinsley singing." She then suggested I bring two friends along to fill the car, so Margaret Williams of Triniti Chapel and a nurse at Cilymaenllwyd Hospital; Michael Thomas, a member of my concert party, Cynthia and myself headed for the Grand Theatre, where Pauline Tinsley, with whom I was friendly, joined us for a meal before the opera. On another occasion, Cynthia, Megan Evans, Sian Evans, Megan Jones, another member of the staff of Ysgol y Strade who died some years ago; Michael Thomas and myself travelled to Swansea again, this time in two cars, to see Pauline Tinsley in Turandot — you see Cynthia was a part of everything. But there was another side to Cynthia Morgan's character. It was one of courage, bravery, grit and determination as we all saw in the last 18 months of her life, and her untimely death at the age of 42. She continued teaching even though she had to go to Singleton Hospital every Friday for treatment. However painful this was she would be back in school on the Monday until Thursday even though her fellow teachers begged her to stay home and rest.

At this time in 1975 Ysgol y Strade was staging The Story of Handel before Christmas. Susan Tiplady was producer and I was responsible for the music. We suggested to Cynthia that we would postpone the production, because of her illness, but she would not hear of it. We then tried to persuade her to let the school hire the costumes for the production. "No way," replied Cynthia. One or two of the ladies on the staff offered to assist Cynthia with the costumes. "No need, I can manage myself. It will be something to keep me going." So Cynthia Morgan won one battle — she was in sole charge of the costumes as wardrobe mistress. We were all worried, because of the strain on her failing health, but she sailed through with a serene and sincere smile on her beautiful face. The costumes were superb. The school gave three performances of the production during the last week of term — Monday, Tuesday and Wednesday evenings, and Cynthia insisted on coming to every performance, although the state of her health really called for plenty of rest. On the Thursday evening of the same week, Form V were holding their annual Christmas party — Cynthia was their form mistress. We all tried to convince her to stay home and rest after a hectic week, but her answer never waivered: "I've promised the children that I would come. I cannot break my promise."

It was a marvellous night. Cynthia was dressed in a beautiful, ballroom gown with a diamond necklace. She really looked like the a fairy princess with her radiant smile. She looked a perfect picture. The pupils of Form V were delighted because they loved Cynthia and although they knew her health was not good they didn't realise that she was a dying woman, and behind that lovely smile was great pain and weakness. After the party Cynthia and I were the last to leave and she insisted she give me a lift home. The following day was the last day of the Christmas term and she was in school as usual. Little did we realise that this would be the last time we would see Cynthia Morgan in Ysgol y Strade. She collapsed with her illness the following evening and was unable to return. The last time I saw Cynthia was in August, 1976 and sadly she died shortly after.

She was a shining light for me in what turned out to be a link with Ysgol Y Strade that spanned a quarter of a century. It was for me a very happy time shared with three dedicated head teachers and a plethora of supportive colleagues. But shining brightest among them all was Cynthia. She is still sorely missed by family, friends and colleagues, but will never be forgotten

Regal and radiant at all times — Her Majesty the Queen Mother as millions will remember her.

Royal Appointment

The Queen Mother

In October 1984, I organised a week's foreign holiday to Florence and Venice for 25 local residents together with some friends from Ammanford. When we arrived in Venice, the Royal Yacht Britannia, was anchored at one of the quays along the Grand Canal. On the Friday morning while Mavis Williams from Ammanford, Lynne Richards, from Tycroes, and myself had gone to La Fenice Opera House to book opera tickets, the others went sightseeing at the Doge's Palace. To their delight they discovered that the Queen Mother was inside, and expected to emerge at any moment. A crowd gathered to watch as she left, and the Llanelli party was near the door, occupying a prime vantage point.

The Queen Mother eventually came out and the Llanelli women began singing God Save The Queen at which Her Majesty stood to attention. After they had finished, she asked where they were from. Margaret Skinner replied: "Llanelli, your Majesty." to which Eirwen Williams and her sister, Nesta Davies, quickly prompted: "Say Swansea because the Queen Mother will not have heard of Llanelli." Hearing this prompted the Royal reply: "Of course I've heard of Llanelli — the home of Welsh rugby, the experts."

Later that afternoon we had rejoined the rest of the party in St Mark's Square and were waiting to see the Queen Mother on a walkabout and visit to St Mark's Cathedral. Nellie Olive Jones and Eluned Davies suggested: "Gethin, we must sing God Save the Queen." I replied that we couldn't sing the National Anthem again as she was on a walkabout and would have to stand still on hearing it. Lynne Richards then suggested singing We'll Keep A Welcome to which we all agreed. Before long we spotted the Queen Mother and started singing. As we came to the chorus — We'll kiss away each hour of hiraeth, when you come home again to Wales — the Queen Mother was right in front of us and did what we expected her not to — she stood still for three or four minutes. When we had finished she turned to her equerry and said: "No wonder they sing so well — they come from Llanelli, Wales."

The following morning Mavis, Lynne and I were on a water bus heading along the Grand Canal towards Venice Lido when the Royal barge passed very close to us. The Queen Mother recognising us gave a delightful wave. When we arrived home in Llanelli we were surprised that everyone knew we had seen her and soon discovered the reason — we had been on BBC TV about five or six times during Kate Adie's reporting of the popular Royal's visit!

Rita Hunter — opera singer with a taste for bara brith.

Bread of Heaven
Rita Hunter

I first met Rita Hunter the great Wagnerian soprano when she sang in the Grand Concert of Llanelli Young Music Lovers' Association at Zion Chapel in April, 1977.
The rich unique voice of the 20-stone, larger-than-life soprano thrilled the Llanelli audience that night especially her renderings of One Kiss, When April Sings, Smiling Through and The Lights of Home.

Afterwards we were all entertained to a meal by councillor and Mrs Mathonwy Jones. Mrs Jones was a very active vice-president of the Young Music Lovers' Association, and she had made some bara brith. Rita enjoyed this and asked for the recipe at which she was duly given a loaf to take back to London. During the concert she sang arias from Aida, Madame Butterfly and Cavelleria Rusticana. The finale was my arrangement of Elgar's Land of Hope and Glory which featured the Aberavon Male Voice Choir with Michael Renier, baritone; Gareth Wyn Thomas, organ and a brass quartet — I was conducting.

I had also been accompanying all night and during the previous six months I had lost over two stone in weight making my suit a little too big for me. As a result, when I lifted up my arms to conduct the finale my trousers began to slip down. I ended up conducting with my right hand, and holding my trousers up with the left. Rita and Michael Renier were dead centre of the pulpit, and could see my plight. After the concert Rita said: "I was dying to laugh, I could hardly keep a straight face." Two years later she published her autobiography and included the anecdote in her book.

She visited Llanelli twice after this, performing in Moriah Chapel and Llanelli Entertainment Centre. In Moriah she sang with Llanelli Male Choir and Garry Nicholas. During the evening, on hearing Garry recite an English poem entitled The Highwayman, in a particularly accomplished manner, she commented: "That boy has talent and should be on the West End stage."

On New Year's Day 1980 Rita was awarded the CBE in the Queen's New Year's Honours List and at the time I was in London with a friend. We were invited to her home for an enjoyable afternoon tea and given a typical, hearty welcome.

In 1982 she emigrated to Sydney, Australia, so it was in Llanelli, that she sang for the last time in Britain. Rita was from Lancashire, but John Thomas, her husband, was born in Aberdare, and being very proud of this Welsh connection she was always signing official documents as Rita Hunter Thomas. When she sang in three and four act Wagnerian operas in Lancashire, legend has it that she would send out a stage hand for fish and chips between acts one and two and then a Lancashire hot pot between acts two and three.

Rita often sang in the Sydney Opera House as well as Covent Garden, Vienna Opera House, the Metropolitan Opera House, New York; La Scala, Milan; San Francisco Opera House, the London Palladium, Royal Albert Hall, Theatre Royal, Drury Lane and the Tower Ballroom, Blackpool. On one occasion Rita, joined myself and a group of Llanelli friends for lunch at the Savoy Hotel, London. When I mentioned that she had sung in all these places, she quickly added: "I have also performed at Moriah and Zion Chapels, Llanelli, and enjoyed singing there to my Llanelli friends as much as I did in any of those other places."

In October 1997 Rita and myself met again for the last time as she died a few years later. Cor Meibion Llanelli were on a tour of Australia and she had been invited to sing as our special guest at Sydney Town Hall. She came out of retirement especially for the concert and sang When April Sings, The lights of Home, My little Welsh Home and a special duet — The Keys of Heaven — with the choir's director and well-known Welsh tenor, Eifion Thomas. Before the concert Eifion and I had been invited to Rita's home for dinner. It was sumptuous — hearty portions of roast chicken, boiled ham and delicious new potatoes followed by apple tart and custard leaving time for just a five-minute rehearsal. It was a wonderful welcome from a wonderful person.

Later, during the performance I remember her saying "I am proud to be a Welsh widow. My husband always told me that you've heard nothing until you've heard a Welsh male voice choir." She turned fully on the stage to face Cor Meibion Llanelli and added: "True, very true."

Eiddwen Mattravers and Mrs Susan Rees — better known to many as Mrs M and Mrs R.

Tucking In
Mrs M and Mrs R

To young pupils of Llanelli Boys' Grammar School, the Tuck Shop at 84 Marble Hall Road — right opposite the school — was a second home. Run by two sisters, Mrs Mattravers and Mrs Rees it was divided into two — ice cream and pop from Mrs M and sweets, chocolates and crisps from Mrs R — what a combination.

These two devout Christian ladies were members of Bethel Baptist Chapel and were very close as sisters. This was demonstrated by Mrs Eiddwen Mattravers, when she nursed her sick sister and ran the shop at the same time. Mrs Susan Rees — or Susie as Mrs Mattravers referred to her — was given great love and care by her sister, and her funeral was from the tuck shop that she loved. During her illness and after her death Mrs Mattravers was helped in the shop by a friend Jenny Williams also of Marble Hall Road.

The Tuck Shop was a favourite place for ministers to meet and chat about religious topics; for teachers to gather to talk about educational matters and for schoolboys to talk about anything that interested them. Many famous people in their day bought everything from ice cream to sweets from Mrs M and Mrs R. Among them were the former Lord Chancellor Elwyn Jones; Clifford Evans, the famous actor; Rachel Roberts the well known Hollywood actress and former wife of Rex Harrison and daughter of Rev. and Mrs Roberts, former minister of Emmanuel Baptist Chapel; Rev. Jubilee Young, Rev. Huw Roberts, Wyn Morris and Dr. Haydn Morris. Mr TV Shaw would always tell his staff when talking about School Prize Day, Christmas Carol Service and St. David's Day eisteddfod: "We must invite Mrs Mattravers and her sister Mrs Rees, they are as important as any members of staff. When the Boys' Grammar School moved to Pwll Mrs Mattravers kept the Tuck Shop open for a few years for the Technical College until she finally retired.

Mrs M and Mrs R never allowed bad behaviour in the shop. A parent once thought they were teachers, because her son had said: "If we do this we'll have a row off Mrs Mattravers." What a marvellous influence these ladies had on us boys. We respected and admired them and secretly loved them very much. Bless you both Mrs M and Mrs R for helping to make the schooldays of so many young boys such a happy period in their lives. In her early days, Eiddwen Mattravers was a very good pianist with many private pupils. She remained a close friend until she died some years ago. I would often call to have a chat with her and Matt especially after Mrs Rees's death — talk would always turn to the Boys' Grammar School, Bethel Chapel and my music.

Cor Meibion Llanelli with conductor Eifion Thomas and accompanist Gethin Hughes.

With heart
Cor Meibion

There has been one period in my half a century of involvement with the music scene in Wales and beyond that I would not have missed at any cost and yet like so much that has occurred in my time at the keyboard — piano or organ — it is something that came about almost by accident.

It is of course my involvement, as accompanist, with Cor Meibion Llanelli. This was not a role that I had intended to take on, but in answer to a plea for help I said I would fill a gap for three months. I remember inquiring at the time exactly what would be entailed in becoming even a stand-in accompanist. One practice a week and just the concerts was what seemed like an acceptable reply.

As time went on I began inquiring whether or not the choir had found a replacement only to be told that though they had interviewed a number of possible candidates none seemed really suitable. Just two weeks before my time was up I was given the

and voice
Llanelli

heartening news that the choir had in fact found the all-elusive accompanist. "At last," said the musical director at the time, Eifion Thomas. "Man or woman?" I inquired. "Oh, a man, yes," said Eifion Thomas. "Would I know him?" I continued, increasingly inquisitively. "Very well," I was told.

"What's his name then," I continued impatiently, just as Eifion was pushing the newly printed programme for the forthcoming concert under my nose. "Oh, No. No. No," I remember saying as the words leapt off the page at me. It clearly stated that the Musical Director was Eifion Thomas an then clearer still — to my eyes at least was what appeared underneath — Accompanist Gethin Hughes.

I continued to protest vociferously, but it was to no avail. "You get on well with everyone and they with you said Eifion. Besides we have a month-long tour of Australia and New Zealand on the cards — and you are coming too." With the prospect of such a musical adventure ahead I gave in. Since then, until July 1, 2006, and my official retirement from the role at a grand concert in the town, ministering to the choir's musical needs has taken up much of my time and provided boundless enjoyment. That initial three months turned into a decade.

One thing is certain — the friendship and camaraderie that exists within the choir is unsurpassed and there is no shortage of tales to tell to prove that. There have also been many interesting incidents that have become the basis of tales that will continue to be told for as long as the choir remains in existence. Among the more entertaining of these is one that originates from the night when the choir was appearing at the Lyric Theatre, Carmarthen with the three tenors: Washington James, Teifryn Rees and Eifion Thomas. The latter of course was also the choir's musical director and had an enormously heavy workload placed upon his shoulders that night both singing and conducting. Everything was progressing well until it came time for the choir to begin its second spot.

The item had been introduced and the lights dimmed as the choir rose to their feet. I lifted my hands in anticipation above the beautiful grand piano ready to begin playing the moment Eifion gave me the signal, but when he turned towards me it was not to begin the piece. Instead, to my amazement, he whispered to me: "What are we singing now Geth?" His mind had, momentarily, gone completely blank. "Llanfair," I whispered back, thinking that would be the end of it. Not so. I realised we had a problem when he turned to me again and said: "How does that go?" There was nothing for it but for me to hum him the first few notes so off I went — doh doh mee mee soh fah mee ray. Fortunately that was enough for him to know where he was and off we went. We had a laugh about it afterwards and often since.

There are many more lighter moments that have punctuated the hard work and dedication that constantly exist behind the polished performances the choir's audiences have witnessed. Not least among these was my meeting with a wombat in an Australian wildlife park in Perth. Eifion and I had to do a TV programme there where we had to feed the

A chorister's eye view of Eifion Thomas, musical director of Cor Meibion Llanelli.

kangaroos and the park's keepers gave me a huge wombat to hold. They placed it in my lap and placed a hat, complete with dangling corks on my head. Now this wombat was docile enough but rather smelly. And while the animal and I parted company readily enough the stink was an altogether different matter and seemed to linger around me for far longer. The smell was a real problem as we had a concert that night and the bus was waiting to leave to take us there, but I had to have an immediate bath and a shower to try to rid myself of the horrible pong.

After that some of the wags in the choir started popping cards under my hotel room door containing spurious messages from the wombat. It was all good clean fun and helped maintain a jovial atmosphere, though quite a long time elapsed after our Australian adventure before the instigators of it all were revealed — former choir member Adrian Hallett spurred on by his wife Jan and mother Dilys. The moment of revelation arrived after a full-blown funeral was held for the wombat while we were performing in Ireland. Such tales are an indication of the kind of fun and humour that is evident in the choir. They are the kind of happenings that help to unite the members. In that way I think we worked well together as accompanist and singers.

There is a tremendous spirit of friendship and camaraderie in the choir, but with around 100 members and officials it is perhaps inevitable that closer friendship groups will develop and I am indebted to those whose closeness has made my time with this fine musical body an even more enjoyable one, not least Terry Morgan, or Terry Bach as he is known, who for the past seven years has provided me with transport to choir practice every Monday and Thursday evening. There are many others whose singular kindnesses to me underline the other side of choir life where members do not simply restrict their support of one another to the performances but extend it to the wider stage of life at large.

It had been my intention to part company completely with the choir this year. That was a daunting thought as it has been such a big part of my life for so long. I knew that I would miss the choir — wombat incidents and all, but I did promise to fill a gap whenever there was need. Much to my delight however I was invited by the choir committee to consider accepting the official post of associate accompanist to provide support when required for my replacement. I needed little encouragement to agree. I can now look forward to the continued company of choir President, Deputy Lord Lieutenant of Carmarthenshire Mr DH Davies OBE., the former chief executive of Dyfed County Council and his wife Menna together with that of choir chairman Mel Harries and his wife Anne. And of course all my old pals.

It will also be a delight to retain contact with the choir at large. I will watch their continued progress closely. Llanelli, like me, can be proud that our town has such an able and accomplished group of singers flying the flag wherever they go. Diolch yn fawr lads!

Frank Phillips, and right, Haydn Jones. Both are seen below with fellow members of staff at Llanelli Boys Grammar School in 1946.

Music Masters
Frank Phillips and Haydn Jones

To many old boys of Llanelli Grammar School the catchphrase 'Every egg a bird, every bird a warbler' is a saying synonymous with Frank Phillips, one of the most well-known and respected teachers at the school. Frank was a terrific personality, an excellent musician with a lively sense of humour.

He was a history teacher and in his final years on the staff, deputy headmaster, but his great love was music, especially Bach and Handel. He taught a few music lessons and was founder-conductor of the school orchestra. Frank had enormous respect for the head of the music department, Haydn Jones. Indeed there was not a greater partnership anywhere in the world than Frank Phillips and Haydn Jones. It was unique

Haydn had a masters degree in music and both he and Frank were former pupils of Sir Walford Davies — Master of the King's Music — when he was lecturer at University College of Wales, Aberystwyth. Not only was Haydn Jones a genius in music, but he was also a great Welsh literary scholar. He loved the Welsh poets and bards and often wrote verses in cynghanedd as well as composing a great deal of music including hymn tunes, anthems, and choral preludes for orchestra and choir, on Welsh hymn tunes Joanna, Groeswen, Caerllyngoed, a selection of old Welsh carols and a selection of old Welsh nursery tunes.

The partnership of Haydn Jones and Frank Phillips was a successful one — they complemented each other to the letter. Haydn was quiet and shy while Frank was full of confidence and humour. Proof of his greatness was a statement he once made to a group of sixth formers: "If I had Haydn Jones's talent as a musician, or Haydn Jones had my cheek — one of us would now be a music lecturer at the Royal Academy."

Frank could draw music out of a stone and possessed a flair for conducting choirs, while it suited Haydn's personality to sit quietly at the piano and act as accompanist. Despite this Frank wouldn't dream of making a big musical decision without consulting Haydn first. Frank was organist and choirmaster of the Parish Church, Llanelli, for many years although his roots were in Soar Chapel, Marsh Street, where his mother worshiped. His mother Ann even sang in the open-air Revival meetings on Bigyn Hill in 1904 and 1905.

The boys in the grammar school would do anything for Frank, even carry him on their shoulders if need be. His favourite expression was "Sing you monkeys, sing until you have a heart attack." His contribution to orchestral music in Llanelli is inestimable — a

Actor Simon Ward with myself when he visited Llanelli for the Young Music Lovers' Association concert in 1983.

labour of love for a long period of time. Among his former pupils were Clifford Evans, Lord Elwyn Jones, Elvet Marks, Roland Morris, Heward Rees, Eric Morris, Wynne S Thomas and many others. Over the years Frank and his wife Gwen fed hundreds of children at their home in Penallt Terrace. This was to save them travelling home to Hendy, Llangennech, Trimsaran or Burry Port, only to return for orchestra practice at 6pm. Gwen would make sandwiches and cakes and feed about 20 children every Thursday like clockwork.

Frank loved Bach. "Give me Bach for breakfast, dinner, tea and supper," he would often say. "Give me a burning crescendo." In laymen's terms meaning build the music up and up to a very loud climax. Haydn's strength on the other hand was quiet genius that was very effective. Every year in the annual carol service at St Alban's Church, Haydn would enlist my assistance at the organ. He only played a harmonium at his chapel — Jerusalem, Penygroes — and did not understand a pipe organ hence the need for me to help him to pull the stops out. On one occasion, deputy headmaster David Roderick, was reading a lesson and Haydn wanted full organ for the carol Hark the Herald Angels Sing. As he was a very stout person, I had to lean over his tummy to bring out the stops on the other side of the organ. After pulling them out and bringing my arm back, my sleeve caught in the bottom row of keys and made a noise like a trumpet fanfare. Haydn was so excitable and nervous, he stood on his feet, treading on the organ pedals generating a thundering sound through the church. Poor Haydn. If looks could kill, we would have both been no more if Frank had his way.

The Rev. JD Williams once remarked: "Haydn Jones is so shy that when he was playing the harmonium in Jerusalem, Penygroes, if he thought a gladioli or a chrysanthemum was peeping at him playing, he'd become a bundle of nerves." What great characters — like many I shall always remember the fantastic duo.

Platform Personality
Simon Ward

The platform of Llanelli railway station was the inauspicious location, on a cold Saturday afternoon in December, 1983 for my first meeting with the actor Simon Ward when he stepped off a train for what was probably his first visit to the town. He was to be the special guest of Llanelli Young Music Lovers' Association at its annual Festival of Carols and as such he gave a splendid performance with readings from Charles Dickens' A Christmas Carol as well as a special poem which Meiriona J Rees, general secretary of Triniti Chapel, had composed especially for him, entitled Christmas.

The festival was held that year at Zion Chapel and when the president of the association, Mr D R Challenor introduced Simon, of Young Winston, fame he described him as one of the greatest young actors and TV personalities of the time and deemed it an honour to welcome him to Llanelli.

Simon of course was later involved with a number of other cinema and TV productions — including Diamonds with John Stride and Taste for Death with Roy Marsden and Fiona Fullerton — although it is for the film Young Winston, much of which was shot on location near Penwyllt in the upper Swansea Valley, that many may possibly still remember him best.

After our station meeting, we made our way to the Bryn Road home of Dorothy Nicholas. Simon received a typical Welsh welcome there, and soon relaxed in the company of Edwina Barney, Madam Peggy Williams, the Blue Riband contralto and Paul Williams, head of the sixth form at Coedcae Comprehensive School. A beautiful meal was rounded off with Dorothy's delicious raspberry pavlova and a fresh fruit salad.

Following the carol service we had another meal in the home of Shirley Edwards and her husband Corris, in Swiss Valley. Fellow guests there included Joy Davies, Daphne Edwards, Mattie Bateman-Morris, Meirion Rees, Joyce McFall and Adrian Hughes. After the meal it was cabaret time. Joy and Daphne, both super sopranos, sang a song each. Mattie Bateman-Morris, sang Daddy Wouldn't Buy Me A Bow-Wow; Susan Tiplady, sixth form head at Ysgol Gyfun y Strade, Adrian Hughes and Joyce McFall, all local amateur actors, recited while Shirley Edwards, head of English at Bryngwyn Comprehensive School rounded off the proceedings with a selection of wartime songs. Simon was quick to appreciate Shirley's talent and said she was good enough to be on the London stage. The following morning Simon headed back to London by train from Swansea. Later that evening he telephoned me and during the conversation remarked

Simon Ward seated with Gethin Hughes and surrounded by Meirion Rees, Adrian Hughes, Joyce McFall and Shirley Edwards at whose home they were pictured during Simon's visit to Llanelli.

"What lovely and marvellous people you have in Llanelli. I felt I had known them all for years — I only wish I had."

Six months later Simon was my guest at the Savoy in London and he reciprocated with a ticket for me at the Playhouse Theatre, Northumberland Avenue, where he was performing, followed by a glass of champagne in his dressing room. Some years ago I met the actor again, this time in the Grand Theatre, Swansea, and we enjoyed a snack together before the play Dangerous Obsession and also had a long chat after. Needless to say his was a brilliant performance.

Playing The Game
The Rugby Boys

Few would deny that rugby plays a big part in the lives of most Llanelli people and if the town has generated its share of stars in the world of music then the same can certainly be said of the rugby field. Among them Phil Bennett and Ray Gravell.

I came to know Phil Bennett in 1979 when he accepted a role as patron of Llanelli Young Music Lovers' Association. For him, at that time, it couldn't get any better. He had captained the Scarlets and then captained Wales to a Triple Crown victory for three consecutive seasons — 1976, 1977 and 1978 and the Grand Slam in 1976 and 1978. To add to that Phil was also captain of the successful British Lions team in 1977. Capped for Wales 29 times, he proved beyond doubt to be one of the greatest outside halves of all time. Phil also made his presence felt on both the cricket and soccer fields from time to time. and later became sports organiser for Llanelli doing as good a job from his office in the Town Hall as he did on the rugby field.

What always amazes me about Phil is his humility, honesty, kindness and down-to-earth friendship. Nothing is too much trouble for him and nothing too little or unimportant. Among a host of public appearances Phil has given several talks to the Young Music Lovers' Association, chaired one of its concerts and read the lessons on three occasions at its carol festival.

There is however one event which stands out in my memory. It occurred in December 1983 when Phil had agreed to read three of his favourite carols at the association's festival in Zion Chapel. At the time he was managing a sports shop in Cowell Street and with his usual humility asked me to pop upstairs to listen to him read the carols to see if it was good enough. He read them perfectly, however, at 5pm on the Saturday evening of the concert I answered the telephone to hear Phil's wife Pat explain that he was working for Radio Wales and had been delayed in Cardiff so would be late arriving for the festival. She added that Phil had said that I wasn't to worry because he would be there by about 8.30pm.

Later, I was at the organ and had informed our president, Raymond Challenor that Phil Bennett would be late arriving, to which he replied that he probably wouldn't come at all. However, he was proved wrong. At 8.25pm precisely I heard the main door of Zion Chapel opening and as I looked through the organ mirror, sure enough Phil appeared, quietly made his entrance and slipped into one of the back seats. Soon the president called him forward and he read most beautifully his three favourite carols: We three

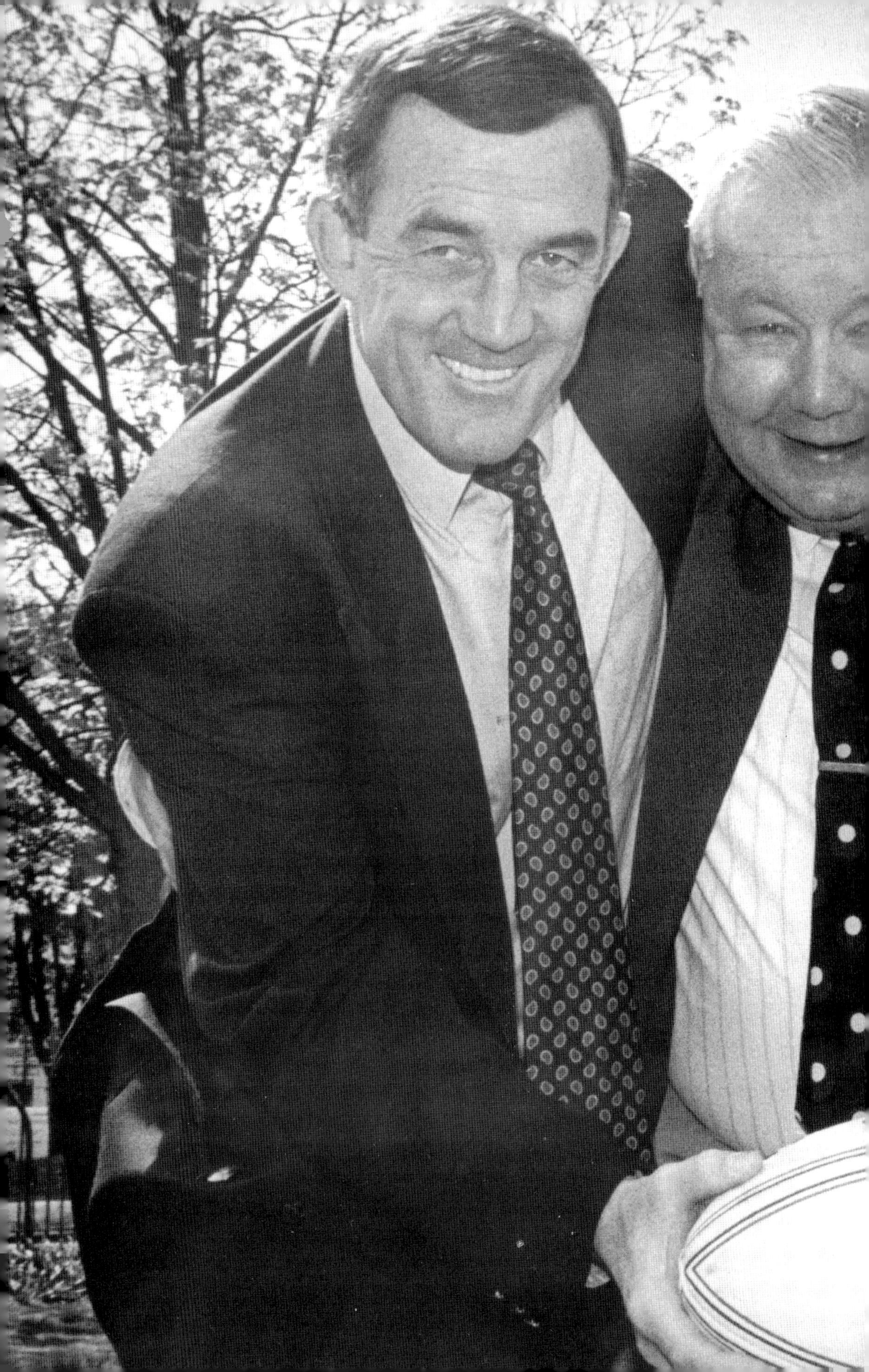

On the ball — a fun moment with rugby stars Phil Bennett and Ray Gravell, two of Llanelli's greatest sporting personalities.

Kings, Once in Royal David's City and O Come All Ye Faithful. When the festival ended we all went into the vestry for tea and sandwiches. It was now about 9.30pm. Soon Phil excused himself from the gathering, informing us that he had to return to the BBC studios in Cardiff to edit that afternoon's match. I spoke to him the following evening and discovered that he had finally arrived back in Llanelli in
2.30am after completing his task. He had made a special return journey from Cardiff just to read those three carols, and not to let me down. When I questioned him about this he told me: "I had promised you, Geth and I felt I just had to keep my promise." What a true and sincere Christian act, what a genuine person. Little things in life mean a lot and this gesture meant a great deal to me and the Young Music Lovers' Association. It demonstrated that Phil Bennett is a sportsman off the field as well as on and was deservedly honoured by the Queen at Buckingham Palace with the OBE.

Another famous Llanelli-grown rugby international I have the pleasure of knowing is Ray Gravell. Capped 23 times for Wales and in the same Triple Crown and Grand Slam winning sides as his old mate and friend Phil Bennett, Ray was an excellent centre forward and a larger than life character. Ray is a fluent Welsh speaker, and a passionate Welshman. The language and culture of his country is very close to his heart. He has a pleasing and sweet singing voice, and since retiring from the rugby field, has made a very successful career on TV and radio as well as in films. He is often asked to compere Welsh Noson Lawen.

Many listeners will be familiar with his regular radio programmes. On one of these he was supposed to give a celebrity concert at our chapel some publicity, but had left the details at home. To my surprise, while listening to Radio Cymru, eagerly awaiting the announcement one August morning, this is what I heard: "Wonderful concert on Friday, September 3 at Triniti Chapel, Llanelli — the international tenor Arthur Davies — Sorry Geth, sorry Geth, I've forgotten the paper with the full details on. I'll read it all out on Thursday. Sorry about this Geth, sorry Geth." What a character. Later Ray published his memoirs in Welsh in a book called simply Grav and a few years ago joined me as an honourary member of the Gorsedd of Bards of the Royal National Eisteddfod of Wales. Ray is now official sword bearer of the Gorsedd and we often share a laugh together while waiting for the procession to begin.

Ray also followed in Phil's shoes when he became Patron of the Llanelli Young Music Lovers' Association. His contribution has been immense and of great value to us all. He is a great Welshman and like Phil and his wife Pat it is an honour for me to count him and his wife Mari as personal friends.

Ivory Queen
Madam Holloway

Without a doubt Madame Florence Holloway can honestly be described as the queen of the ivories. She was, after all, one of Wales's most renowned, capable and fascinating accompanists. Not only were skills as an accompanist excellent, but she was also an unique artist.

Florence Evans was born in Portsmouth, but at the age of seven moved with her family to Myrtle Terrace, Llanelli. She married Doddie Holloway of the well-known Llanelli garage family and lived in Andrew Street. She gained her teacher's diploma, her ARCM and LRAM and taught for a period in a temporary capacity at Llanelli Girls' Grammar School. She taught hundreds of pupils to play the piano, gave voice lessons privately at home, and became very well known as an accompanist in eisteddfodau across Wales.

Madam Holloway was the accompanist of Llanelli Choral Society, with Edgar Thomas as conductor, when it won first prize at the National Eisteddfod in 1937. Florence added a far more unusual first to her tally later however when she became one of the first women in Wales to drive heavy lorries and trucks. She did so for Holloway's Garage during the Second World War. People often wondered how Madam Holloway was able to keep her fingers so nimble and agile and tackle the role of driving a lorry, but she simply wore protective gloves. She recalled once she was driving a huge truck down to Barry Docks during the war, and when she arrived at the dock gates, four men exclaimed in amazement and unison: "It's a woman!"

Such was her standing that some of the greatest artists in the world are known to have asked for Madam Holloway as their accompanist. I remember the first time I saw her perform was in a 1943 celebrity concert at the Regal Cinema, Llanelli. Sadly, her husband Doddie had died and the funeral had been three days before. Florence was devastated and decided she couldn't go through with the concert and face an audience, so she informed the organisers. The soloists on that evening were Isobel Baillie, Mary Jarred, Henry Wendon and Robert Easton. Isobel Baillie, talking on behalf of her fellow artists, informed the organisers that they would not sing in Llanelli unless Madam Holloway would accompany them. No other accompanist would do. They were in a tight spot, so they implored Florence to change her mind.

Eventually her in-laws intervened, and begged her to play, saying it would be Doddie's wish that she should carry on and play. Reluctantly she agreed, but insisted that the piano was turned so that she would not face the audience and that she would not

Madam Florence Holloway.

acknowledge them or take a bow. I was in the audience that night with my mother and could sense the sympathy of the audience with her grief. She wore a black full-length dress with a narrow band of red across her short sleeves, and when she walked across the stage, lifted her head upright and turned it from the auditorium towards the back of the stage. Florence Holloway was a supreme artist and well known for her beautiful and elegant evening gowns. She once told me she was playing for a famous Italian soprano.

She was accompanying her to sing The Bell Song. In this very famous solo, the soprano sings unaccompanied, then there is the sound of bells, which is then echoed by the piano. However, both Florence and the soloist got into a terrible mess and the artist became very upset, and said to Flo: "No! No! No! You are playing my bells, and I am singing your bells!" Eventually they tried it again and it was perfect.

Florence Holloway also played for many years at the Urdd National Eisteddfod, the National Eisteddfod, Llangollen International Eisteddfod and for Llanelli Ladies Choir. She had her own glee party and broadcast frequently on radio, often recording at Triniti Chapel. She would support everyone, and praise other musicians. She would often phone my mother after I had played in a concert and say: "Mrs Hughes, you can be very proud of your son tonight, Gethin played superbly."

She was a wonderful friend. Once, the night before I was due to play in a concert, I became panic-stricken. I just couldn't play the sextuplets in Eri tu', the famous baritone aria from Verdi's A Masked Ball. There is a series of six notes and I've only got five fingers! I was stumped. The only solution was to phone the great woman herself which I did. She answered in her beautiful speaking voice giving her Ammanford number and finishing with: "Florence Holloway speaking." I told her my problem, and immediately she shared a valuable and never-to-be-forgotten trick of the trade. "Darling, second thumb under 2,1,3,4,5 up and then down 5,4,3,2,1,2 and second over. You try it my love, and all the best for tomorrow night," were her words. I did try it and am not afraid to admit that Florence saved the day. When I looked at her in her seat in the gallery of Moriah Chapel during the concert she was beaming all over her face and when she caught my eye gave me the thumbs up.

She remarried around 1950 to DJ Morgan of Ammanford, and moved there from Llanelli. She often told me that she never really settled in Ammanford. Although she lived there for 30 years it seems her heart was still in Llanelli where she had lived for around half a century. She came to town every Thursday for more than 25 years and taught pupils in the parlour of Mr and Mrs Williams in Andrew Street. Their daughter Joan Lewis was conductor of Bryncoch Male Voice Choir and head of music in Cefn Saeson Comprehensive School, Cimla, Neath.

At the age of 70, Florence agreed to become one of four founder vice-presidents of Llanelli Young Music Lovers' Association, a post she held until her death in 1987 at the age of 87. Not only was she a marvellous musician, but also a magnificent prose reader and actress. Her Bible reading was always one of the highlights of the association's carol festival every year. She was excellent on any panel game, and a prolific speaker.

She was never known as Mrs Morgan or Florence Holloway-Morgan, but always as Madam Holloway. To her friends, and I was privileged to be one, she was just Flo.

Jack Warner — better known to millions as TV policeman Dixon of Dock Green.

Family of Fame
Elsie and Doris Waters

One of the most famous showbusiness families in Britain at one time was the Waters family — three of its six children became household names. Elsie and Doris became legends in their lifetime as the characters Gert and Daisy while brother Jack became one of TV's most famous policemen — Dixon of Dock Green.

It all started when Elsie and Doris — their other siblings were Arthur, Bernard and Leslie — were very young. Elsie who played violin to Doris's piano suggested she should sing a song or two while her sister accompanied. Soon they started writing songs — Elsie the words and Doris the music.

One day they were cutting a record and after completing one side, found themselves at a loss on what to record on the other. Elsie suggested a wedding theme and so they wrote their first big song, Wedding Bells, about two cockney charwomen watching a wedding. Doris said: "We must have names, so I'll call you Gert — because I like the name." Elsie replied: "I'll call you Daisy — because there's always a Daisy among us." Thus the characters of Gert and Daisy were born to live on for 50 years as superstars.

As their popularity grew Elsie and Doris moved away from performances for WIs, Rotary and Soroptimist clubs and progressed in a big way through music hall, variety and radio. Soon they were performing all over the world — America, Canada, Australia, New Zealand, South Africa, India and Burma.

They appeared twice in a Royal Command Performance show, once at the Palladium, once at the Coliseum, and also for three weeks at Windsor Castle during the war. Their fellow stars were Laurel and Hardy, Vera Lynn, Arthur Askey and many more. Gert and Daisy even helped Prime Minister Winston Churchill and Lord Woolton, Minister of food and rations during the war years. They toured Britain singing songs about rationing which pleased the two politicians very much such as:

"Here's a recipe from the kitchen front;
Please try it, don't be lazy;
If it all goes wrong, we'll bear the brunt;
Your old friends, Gert and Daisy"

The sisters could be regularly heard in two radio series — Petticoat Lane and Gert and Daisy's Working Party — and remained at the top of their profession for over 50 years,

To Esther
with love

Elsie
(Jerb)

Elsie and Doris Waters dressed for the parts of Gert and Daisy that brought them nationwide fame.

a reign that only came to an end when Doris — Daisy — died. Their brother Jack changed his named to Jack Warner, to avoid accusations of cashing in on his sisters' success, and became famous as TV's Dixon of Dock Green. I had known him for some time, but not the girls, though I had seen them perform when I was only 14, at the Pier Pavilion, Llandudno, with Anne Ziegler and Webster Booth.

Elsie, Doris and Jack were patrons of my concert party for many years, and after Jack's death Elsie invited me to visit her at her home in Sussex which I did on a number of occasions, always receiving a warm welcome. She had a fund of stories from her long career and was always keen to share them.

On one occasion Elsie was a guest in the Royal Box at the Royal Albert Hall for a Burma Reunion, with Prince and Princess Michael of Kent and Lady Slim. While Elsie was talking, she heard rapturous applause coming from the audience. Eventually Lady Slim had to prompt Elsie: "You'd better stand up dear, it's you they're applauding."

Elsie told me a lovely tale of how, when the family were young she and Doris, their four brothers, father and mother would join in an orchestral and choral ensemble around the piano after a Sunday evening service. She said: "I would play the violin, Jack the viola, my father's secretary would play the piano, my brother Bernard would also play violin, and the other boys would sing. Doris would play the tubular bells though she would hit the wood more often than she would hit the bells." One evening everybody had finished playing, except Bernard who was still playing the violin. When Elsie informed him that they had finished playing he asked her what everyone had been playing. "We've been playing The Yeoman of the Guard," said Doris. "Oh, sorry," said Bernard. "I've been playing The Mikado."

Once, after a lovely meal in Elsie's house, I sat at her beautiful white piano, and sang probably the most famous signature tune in the world: Daisy, Daisy, give me your answer do, before Elsie sang a beautiful song which she and Doris had written. To me it sums up the charisma that was the Waters family — pals.

Friendship is certainly something Elsie and Doris placed much emphasis on as one of Gert and Daisy's frequently heard and often repeated verses underlines:

> **'As pals we meet, as pals we part, as pals we meet again,**
> **A handshake true, a smile or two,**
> **When things go wrong I can count on you,**
> **Old friends are best, they stand the test,**
> **They're the same in the sun, wind or rain,**
> **So, as pals we meet, as pals we part,**
> **as pals we meet again!'**

Clean Easy
Dai and Jenny Ty Capel

Dai and Jenny Ty Capel were among the best known and well-liked characters in the New Dock area of Llanelli. They were caretakers of Triniti Chapel for a considerable time — she for 42 years until she died, while Dai carried on for a further 15 years with the help of his sister Olwen.

Dai — David William Thomas — was born in Stafford Street, Llanelli, the eldest child of John and Mary Hannah Thomas. While serving in the Army during the First World War he was stationed in Glasgow and when he returned home in 1922 he brought with him a bride — Janet Haddow. It was a brave step for Janet to leave her beloved and bonnie native Scotland in 1922, but she soon made herself at home in Llanelli and by the time of her death in 1965 she was a natural Welsh person. She quickly learned Welsh and was even heard on BBC Radio relating how she had started learning the language — halen is salt, bara is bread and so on. It must have worked and very well, for she could recite Welsh poems and hymns in the Penny Reading and Fellowship in Triniti Chapel, where she and Dai were faithful members. They became the caretakers in 1925 and remained so until their deaths. Jenny soon became Jenny Ty Capel (Jenny Chapel House) throughout the New Dock area. With a sweet voice she sang with great feeling, but will be remembered best for her singing of popular Gracie Fields songs.

As a caretaker David Thomas was second to none. He looked after the boilers for more than 30 years, wheeling barrows full of fuel from the coal house to the boiler room. On Christmas Eve, Dai never went to bed. Instead he slumbered in the chair keeping an eye on the boiler for the 6am morning service on Christmas Day. For years he cut the vast boundary lawns with a scythe until finally the chapel provided him with a lawn mower. He also trimmed the trees, and painted the external doors — he was a superb caretaker who was really dedicated to the task he seemed to love so much.

Ministers who visited Triniti knew Jenny well. Among them one of Wales's greatest ministers and hymn-writers, Dr. Moelwyn Hughes. In the chapel's anniversary meetings he was guest preacher. Jenny was at her usual post in the lobby, listening to the people as they moved out to the street. As a group of Capel Newydd elders passed her, she overheard them slightly criticising Moelwyn Hughes's sermon. They thought that it was brilliant but that he was rather quiet at times so that they missed some of its pearls and gems. Jenny thought it a pity that he was being condemned and decided to talk to him about this before Sunday's evening service. As she was helping the choir to sing an

Jenny Ty Capel. She embraced Wales, its people, culture and language. Below: A rare photograph of David Thomas — Dai Ty Capel.

anthem, she had to pass through the minister's room to go up to the choir loft. Dr. Hughes was sitting in the room and, as she passed him Jenny said: "Come here a minute, I've got a bone to pick with you." Dr. Hughes replied: "What is it Mrs Thomas fach?" She continued: "Well, I heard a group of Capel Newydd elders talking in the lobby last night and they said that you were preaching well, but thought it a pity that you were so quiet that they missed your pearls and gems. Now say your piece louder tonight, — we're paying you enough for anniversary services."

After saying her piece she moved up to the choir loft to sit at the side of the organ, in full view of the vast congregation — chapels were packed in those days. As the service proceeded, Dr. Hughes came to his sermon and his text: Ye are the light of the World. He was very quiet and Jenny started talking to herself: "I might as well have spoken to the wall — he hasn't listened to me, one single bit." As she was placing a Mint Imperial in her mouth to keep her throat moist for the anthem, Dr. Hughes repeated his text, but a little louder, before repeating it for a third time when he yelled out the text and turned in the pulpit to face Jenny and said: "Now then Mrs Thomas fach, is that loud enough for you?" She had such a shock, she swallowed the mint.

On another occasion, after scrubbing the vestry one Thursday, she was watching people coming in to Fellowship and telling everybody to wipe their feet. One member remarked that she would wipe her feet, as they were dirty, to which Jenny replied: "No, no, your feet are not dirty, it's your shoes that are dirty." What a colourful character. Those same words had been spoken to her some years earlier and now she was issuing them forth herself.

As a member of my concert party for 11 years, Jenny was well-loved by audiences all over Wales. She took great pleasure in being billed as the Scottish lassie singing in Welsh and lead the party in her version of Macnamara's Band — Highland Jenny's Band — the chorus would go like this:

'When the drums go bang and the cymbals clang and the horns all blaze away
John Griffiths plays the old bassoon, while Meiriona the pipes will play
So leglsy, peglsy, toodles and flute my word it's something grand
and a credit to old Scotland, boys is Highland Jenny's Band.'

Jenny even appeared on the BBC's This Is Your Life programme with Eamon Andrews. The subject was my uncle — Councillor John Griffiths, a former Mayor of the town and Jenny's duet partner in my concert party with the song Madam Will You Walk? When she died she left a great gap in her home and our community.

Dai was a brilliant elocutionist and actor, in both Welsh and English. His marathon Welsh poems were Bydd Yn Ddyn, Yr Iesu; and Gwron Econima, and his masterpiece was the English poem Pack of Cards. All his recitations were filled with tension and drama. The Pack of Cards was his own version and at one point in the recitation he talked about the 10 virgins — five had enough oil for their lamps, and five did not have enough oil — five wise virgins and five foolish virgins. However, Dai's version was "Five were wise, five were otherwise."

Dai acted in Welsh with the Triniti Chapel Drama Company, Cwmni'r Hafan. His fellow actors in many performances included Lewis Griffiths, Herbert Leyshon, Jack Jones, Billy Williams, Johnny Vaughan, Olive Thomas, Mary and Maggie James, Mary Hopkins and my mother — then Blodwen Davies. The dramas he acted with Cwmni'r Hafan included Dwywaith yn Blentyn, Cyfrinach y Fasged Frwyn, Change, Peleni Pitar and many others.

In later years, he acted with Miss Every and Mrs Lizzie Moss Lloyd in Cobbler's Wax and with Mrs May Bevan Smedley in Collier's Log but his masterpiece was with the Welsh section of Llanelli Little Theatre — Minnie Morgan's production of Canmlwydd or Hundred years old. He portrayed superbly the frail, 100 year old Papa Juan with May Bevan Smedley, Margretta Every and Gwladys Thomas. Dai's mother had embroidered a special nightcap and smoking jacket especially for his portrayal of Papa Juan.

In August 1951 the company was competing in the National Eisteddfod and Dai's mother was on her death bed. She adored her son and begged him not let the company down. Dai heeded her wishes and they won first prize. Mary Hannah Thomas waited to see her son, and speak to him on his return. As soon as she heard the good news of the win from his lips she smiled, whispered "Good Boy." and peacefully passed away.

Dai followed in his father's footsteps, and became an elder in Triniti Chapel. His father John Thomas was a very colourful character. Every Christmas morning he would go out onto the pavement in Stafford Street and shout at the top of his voice: "Happy Birthday, Lord Jesus." Mrs Thomas would run after him and tell him to be quiet and come indoors. John Thomas would reply: "Mary Hannah fach, the devil is advertising his wares so must we as Christ's followers. Happy Birthday Lord Jesus."

Dai who died in 1983 took part in two musicals with my concert party and in one of these productions, Ahoy There, he sang a Scottish love duet with his wife Jenny. He loved the old Scottish entertainers, Will Fyfe and Sir Harry Lauder, and also the great Scottish poet Robbie Burns, but he had a passion too for Welsh hymns, sermons, and readings of the Bible especially the second chapter of the Book of Acts. After Jenny and Olwen died, Dai lived on his own. Most Saturday afternoons I would go across to have a run on the organ, and the ritual was to call at Ty Capel afterwards and join Dai in a cup of tea, a piece of cake and some friendly banter.

Sweet Songsters
The great contraltos

Wales has always taken pride of place as far as contralto soloists are concerned, and Llanelli can lay claim to a major slice of them. As a young child growing up in Llanelli I I soon came to know about contraltos — my mother and grandmother and Auntie Gertie had beautiful alto voices and sang in Triniti Chapel choir. There the lead contralto was Sarah Annie Wangland who possessed a rich and fulsome voice. Another Triniti member, Mary Esther Jenkins of Tyisha Road, became an international contralto, singing in concerts far and wide. She was a pupil of Madam Clora Novello Davies, Ivor Novello's mother.

I soon came to hear and instantly recognise the rich contralto voices of Vera Tiley-James, Violet Badger-Davies and of course, heard Gwyneth Beynon sing in many local concerts and eisteddfodau — her hallmark solo was Craig yr Oesoedd. They were all good, but Llanelli could go a step further and produce Blue Riband contraltos too, particularly in the person of Madam Sal Thomas, Llwynhendy. She sang Jezebel in the operatic version of Elijah by Capel Als choir with great success and on the same occasion gave an equally contrasting performance of the Angel singing the beautiful aria O Rest in the Lord.

Sal Thomas was a superb contralto, a lovely lady, and a very faithful member of Berea, Bynea. I was privileged to accompany her in a concert at Triniti Chapel in 1954, and enjoyed every moment of this great honour. Sadly she died in her nineties, but Llwynhendy will always be able to look back with pride on its links with such a tremendous singer.

Another golden voiced contralto — a voice almost like a bass, certainly like an organ — was Madam Gwen Downing-Jones, caretaker and worshipper at Zion Chapel for many years. Gwen was also a Blue Riband winner who sang in many concerts with top line artists like Gwen Catley, Isobel Baillie, David Lloyd and many others. She sang the contralto part in Verdi's Requiem and Hymn of Praise at Capel Newydd and Tabernacle. I first heard Gwen sing at a concert in Dock Chapel. She gave a superb performance of The Lost Chord. Although I was only seven years old I remember saying to my mother as I sat beside her: "This lady has a beautiful voice Mammy." Gwen was also a member with Eddie and Annie Watkeys of the famous Llan Gang which performed all over Wales. I have played for Gwen on many occasions, but my favourite song of hers was The Wandering Player. I am proud to say however that four of Wales's greatest contraltos are also connected with the Llanelli area — Lynne Richards, of Tycroes ;

Lynne Richards, left, and Marian Roberts.

Lavina Thomas.

Peggy Williams.

Peggy Williams, of Trimsaran; Lavina Thomas and Margaret Morris-Bowen. Lynne Richards will always be known by people all over Wales as Madam Lynne Richards, Tycroes. This complimentary title is only given to singers of renown in the principality, the most famous of course being the legendary Madam Adelina Patti.

Born and bred in Tycroes, Ammanford, where she still lives, Lynne Richards, did not have to change her surname when she married Bryn Richards, himself an excellent musician and very good accompanist. Lynne was a teacher in Manchester, Cardiff and finally in Llanedi. She won the opera contralto solo competition three times in the Llangollen International Eisteddfod and also the contralto solo in the National Eisteddfod several times, finally winning the Blue Riband in Ystradgynlais in 1954. Lynne has performed with some of the world's most famous and accomplished singers including Pauline Tinsley, Forbes Robinson, Elizabeth Harwood, Arthur Davies Isobel Baillie and Stuart Burrows.

Former local education officer W Harold Evans once said in a public committee meeting that Lynne Richards had sung with the Ammanford Choral Society and three London artists. "Madam Lynne Richards was equal to the London artists, though to be perfectly honest she was better." I first heard her in a concert at Capel Als in 1951, with Llwynhendy bass Harding Jenkins and the Hywel Girls Choir. She was quite superb. I then heard her a few months later at the Public Hall, Llanelli in a dramatic presentation of Handel's Messiah with Capel Als Choral Society conducted by Dr. Haydn Morris with Betty Tovey, soprano, Euryl Coslett, tenor and Harding Jenkins, bass. Lynne was superb, her rich, dark contralto voice was particularly thrilling in the aria He Was Despised.

I first came to know Lynne on a personal level in November 1955 when I was playing in a concert at Capel Als for Richard Rees the Blue Riband bass singer. The main attraction was the international oratorio soprano Isobel Baillie, who had her own accompanist; Lynne was also taking part and Bryn her husband was going to play for her. In the rehearsal Bryn heard me play for Richard Rees and immediately told Lynne: "There is no need for me to play for you, this young man is excellent, he has a brilliant future." Lynne turned to me and asked me to accompany her as well as Richard Rees. I was then only 20 and delighted that the concert was a huge success.

Since that distant day she and I have been the greatest of friends. She has been with a group of us on continental holidays to Venice, Vienna, Amalfi and Rome and several times to London, including Covent Garden Opera House and the Savoy Hotel. She is a wonderful friend and superb cook — every trip we went on Lynne would bring a box of delicious home made Welsh cakes. She was good fun too and on one occasion Mavis Williams, Gary Nicholas, Lynne and myself climbed to the top of the Leaning Tower of Pisa, where without warning she sang out Cymru Fach, her rich voice flowing over Pisa.

In my mother's funeral Lynne made history by singing solo during the service at the house. She sang Y Nefoedd (Heaven) with such conviction and tenderness, that she touched everyone present. One of the bearers told me afterwards, when he heard Lynne Richards sing: "I was gripped, I felt I was on a higher level, I felt I was in the presence of God Almighty."

Again like Lynne, Peggy Williams is always known by the courtesy title of Madam Peggy Williams, Trimsaran and is one of Wales's most famous singers and soloists. She ran the village post office with her husband Elis and is one of only five singers in Wales who have won the coveted Blue Riband on two occasions — in 1960 at the Cardiff National Eisteddfod and then, four years later in Swansea. In addition Peggy has the unique honour and accolade of being the only singer in Wales to win the open contralto or open mezzo-soprano solo, in the Llangollen International Eisteddfod for 10 consecutive years — a brilliant achievement. She is a member of the well known and highly respected Williams family, Trimsaran, many more of whom have acquitted themselves well in the competitive world of Welsh eisteddfodau.

Madam Peggy Williams also served as conductor of Trimsaran Ladies Choir and for some time was in charge of the singing in Sardis Chapel, in the village and has conducted Womens' Institute Choirs in special festivals. A few years ago she sang a principal role with Burry Port Opera. Like Lynne, Peggy too, has been a friend of mine for many years. She sang in my mother's memorial service at Triniti Chapel in January 1987, with Sybil Perrott at the organ.

On a lighter note she was one of the party of 30 of us who visited Rome for a holiday a few years ago and I have always enjoyed Peggy's company at all times. One of my greatest musical memories is when Peggy and Lynne Richards were joined by another fantastic Blue Riband Contralto — Lavina Thomas, of Llandeilo — to sing Craig yr Oesoedd at Tabernacle Chapel in May, 1992 — it was Lynne's last performance as a soloist. What a reception these three giants of song received from the audience and what a superb performance they gave in return. To me they were Wales's female answer to Domingo, Pavarotti and Carreras!

Mention must also be made however of the youngest of these great contraltos — National winner Margaret Morris-Bowen, another fine-voiced singer who we can be proud to say hails from the Llanelli area.

Don't Kill Mother
Pauline Tinsley

One of the most dramatic and dynamic of British opera stars in my estimation is undoubtedly Pauline Tinsley, whose outstanding voice has thrilled audiences all over the world. Born in Manchester, this warm, generous lass from Lancashire won the hearts of thousands of opera lovers. She trained at the city's college of music, gaining her LRAM credentials as a piano performer, but it was as a singer, a tremendous, dramatic soprano, that she was to make her name.

I first heard Pauline sing in the Grand Theatre, Swansea in 1966. On that evening she gave a superb performance of Lady Macbeth, one of the many roles she is famous for. Robert Edwards, a teacher friend, was with me on that occasion and we were both floored by the performer's excellent singing and superb acting, especially in Lady Macbeth's sleep-walking scene. At the end of the performance the audience gave her a standing ovation. The applause was tumultuous. She was overjoyed at the reception and was called back repeatedly for more curtain calls.

Pauline Tinsley — a tremendous, dramatic soprano.

A few weeks later, the headmaster of Ysgol y Strade at the time, Raymond Challenor, allowed me to invite Pauline Tinsley to the school to talk and sing for the pupils. "I don't think she'll come Gethin," he said. "An artist of her calibre will want a high fee, but there's no harm in asking." No-one was more surprised than Mr Challenor when I informed him that Pauline had accepted my invitation to sing in the school hall in May when she would be appearing with the Welsh National Opera in Cardiff.

On the allotted day she came down by train, arriving in time for lunch at the school and a short rehearsal with me at the piano before giving a superb recital and talk for the pupils in the school hall. She then dashed back to Cardiff to sing the role of Abigail in

Pauline Tinsley in the famous sleepwalking scene from Macbeth.

Nabucco that evening. The children of Strade school were eating out of her hands and enjoyed every single moment of her visit.

The experience was repeated two years later when Denis Jones was headmaster. This time Pauline brought with her a very expensive evening dress and cape trimmed with ermine, and changed her recital. This added a definite touch of class to her performance. Mr Jones, thanking her at the end of the performance, described her recital as "Par excellence." He was right, she is a truly great artist. On both of these occasions she refused emphatically to accept any financial recompense with the reason: "I enjoy performing for children, it is my pleasure, and it may encourage them to enjoy opera."

Pauline again came to sing for the school in 1970, this time in a public concert at Capel Als after the evening service on Sunday. The chapel was packed to capacity and the event was a huge success. Soon she, her family, and I became great friends and have remained so to this day.

Pauline tells many a story from her long career, but one of the funniest involves her son John, who was only four when he watched his mother perform in the opera Nabucco. In one scene the Assyrians had their arrows aimed to shoot her when a little voice wafted over the audience "Don't kill my mother." Later, when Pauline was singing the role of the Queen of Egypt in Rossini's Moses, she was eight months' pregnant with her daughter Julia who, as a result, became known as the Moses baby. Pauline has sung all the greatest operatic soprano roles and among her greatest successes have been Turandot, Aida, Elecktra, Tosca, Lady Macbeth and Leonora. She sang and acted the sleepwalking scene from Macbeth at a Royal Command Performance for the Duke of Edinburgh at Southwark Cathedral and was personally complimented on her performance by the Duke.

She later performed the same routine at Moriah Chapel, Llanelli, with myself at the organ in a concert jointly organised by Coedcae and Strade schools. Also appearing on that occasion were Llanelli Male Choir; Hugh Davies and Elwyn Harries, duets; Susan Tiplady and Paul Williams, dramatic readings and Haldon Evans, trumpet. When she finished her performance the audience in Moriah gave this lovely lady a well-deserved standing ovation.

Another visit to Llanelli came in April 1986, when she sang in Capel Newydd with Arthur Davies and Rhymney Silurian Male Choir. On that occasion she was suffering from attacks of asthma, but with the grit and determination of a true professional carried on and gave a remarkable performance. Pauline once invited me, the late Elsie Jones, former Welsh teacher at Llanelli Girls' Grammar School and Vera Tiley-James, to tea with her in Swansea, before a performance of Nabucco. Her humility is something else for which she is widely known. On one occasion she knelt to talk to 82-year-old soprano Mary Williams who always spoke of Pauline as 'the tops.'

Emmie Brown — her piano instruction was friendly, but firm.

Musical Magic
Emmie Brown

I owe most of my musical ability — certainly that on the piano — to Miss Emmie Brown, formerly of Richard Street, Llanelli. She taught me piano and music theory for 11 years and helped coach me for O and A-level music. I certainly missed her friendly, but firm, instruction when I left Llanelli Boys' Grammar School to study at Trinity College, Carmarthen.

Emmie Brown was not only an excellent musician, but an outstanding character and personality. Her father, James Brown, was a partner in the well-known local contracting firm of Brown, Thomas and John and her mother, Clara, was a true and charming lady. When I began having piano lessons, one of the highlights for me was to be allowed to go out to the kitchen to have a chat with Mrs Brown and share a biscuit or piece of chocolate with Emmie's sister-in-law Lil.

Emmie had three brothers — Bill, Allan and Roy. Bill was an elder in Greenfield Chapel where Emmie and Allan were also faithful members. Allan and his wife Ethel were tragically killed in a car accident near Gorseinon. Esme was the only niece, and pride of place in the centre of the top of the piano was devoted to her photograph along with a metronome — the only two items on her treasured piano.

Emmie Brown was an excellent teacher, firm and strict but, kind and human. She never gave me a new piece of music to play without playing it herself first to show me how it should be played. Another of her policies was never to progress to a new piece of music before perfecting the current one. When preparing for examinations, she was very kind, and I received lessons every day of the week, including Sunday for a fortnight prior to the day of the test, free of charge. They would last for 15 minutes, but were invaluable. She was so thorough and a perfectionist. The day of the examination was an important one for all of Miss Brown's pupils when it was a case of all aboard the train to Swansea. Examinations of the Royal School of Music were held at that time at Swansea Museum. Every entrant had to walk across a large hall to the piano near one of the vast windows, passing on their way a large stuffed elephant. After the exam was over we would all go, parents included, to have lunch at Woolworth's High Street cafeteria before boarding the Mumbles Train for a trip to the resort. Miss Brown would be firmly in charge at all times.

Before my Grade V Examination, Miss Brown was listening to me playing one of the pieces called Lamb's Frolic. Suddenly she shouted: "No, no, Gethin it's more like an elephant's stampede than a lamb's frolic. You are far too heavy — you must loosen your wrists and have a lighter touch. I want lambs not elephants." She then loosened my wrists tapping them lightly on the piano.

When I started having lessons at the age of eight, Emmie Brown, said to my mother: "I will not make a machine of Gethin, simply teaching him to play a few selected pieces to concert perfection, but he will sight read and learn to accompany." How indebted I am to her for that, because the ability to do that is far more valuable than just being able to play party pieces. I can remember when I was studying for my music O-level, Frank Phillips, music master at Llanelli Boys' Grammar School, asked if I had piano lessons with Mr James Bevan, as most Llanelli young musicians did. I informed him that I was a pupil of Emmie Brown to which he replied: "Good old Emmie, she's turned out a musician, not just a pianist." What a compliment from someone who himself was one of Llanelli's musical giants. She was paid a further compliment many years later, when the BBC conductor and former conductor of the National Youth Orchestra of Wales, Dr. Clarence Raybould enquired who had taught me to play. When told, he replied: "Whoever the lady was, she definitely knew the technique of piano teaching and general musicianship."

Emmie, who died in 1966, had exquisite taste and always dressed elegantly. Every summer in Greenfield's Sunday School anniversary, the piano would be wheeled into the chapel for her to play for the children, because as the minister at the time, Rev. BJ Davies often said: "Miss Brown has such a lovely touch on the piano, and has such a way with children." When she died in 1966, Llanelli lost one of its great musical personalities. Hundreds of former piano pupils will, I'm sure, be grateful for her endeavours. This one certainly is to this day, and along with the kind and generous Haydn Henshaw who later taught me how to master the organ has to be one of the biggest musical influences in my formative years.

It was a delight to play the organ at Salisbury Cathedral during July, 1996.

Delightful Discovery
Vilna Challenor

In July, 1965 I was appointed music teacher at Ysgol y Strade. Raymond Challenor was the headmaster at the time, and he invited me to the home he shared with his wife Vilna in Chapman Street to chat about my teaching duties. It was a Saturday afternoon and I expected to be talking shop for about an hour before heading home. Not So! I was there for nearly five hours. We talked about school matters for about an hour, and then I was introduced to Mrs Challenor, who had prepared a lovely afternoon tea, the first of very many meals I was to share with them. I started my duties in Strade School in September 1965 and it wasn't long before I made a very rewarding discovery — Vilna Challenor possessed a most glorious contralto voice, and was a beautiful soloist.

Vilna was born in Burry Port and her father Ben Francis was the organist of the English Congregational Church there for many years. Vilna eventually followed in his footsteps and also became its organist. She had received singing lessons from Arthur Davies who was organist and choirmaster of Mount Pleasant Baptist Chapel, Swansea for many years. she also received voice training from Madam Edgar Thomas and Madam Florence Holloway.

In domestic life Vilna was behind her husband every inch of the way. After leaving Ysgol y Strade he became headmaster of Llanelli Girls Grammar School — the first man to hold the position — and finally he took the lead role at Bryngwyn Comprehensive. Vilna was a superb cook and when Raymond was head of Llanelli Girls' Grammar and Bryngwyn comprehensive schools, she helped cook refreshments for the guests at school prize days for years — "To help the domestic science departments," — was her reason, because in Vilna's words "there is a lot of work and pressure on teachers today, especially domestic science teachers."

This delightful woman was a member of my concert party for 10 years and gave pleasure to hundreds of people with her lovely voice and personality. She sang in a concert at Capel Newydd with many well known vocalists including Richie Thomas, tenor and Richard Rees, bass and another in the Presbyterian Chapel with Janice Davies-Rees, soprano; Teifryn Rees, tenor and Evan Lloyd, bass. Vilna was a member of Llanelli Amateur Operatic Society for a few years and sang a principle role in The Gondoliers. She sang for many years with Bryngwyn School's staff choir, under the direction of Sally Arthur — and returned to help the choir for a few years after Raymond had retired. Vilna was an attentive hostess and entertained many celebrities at her home including well-known operatic baritone Terence Sharpe and world famous

Vilna Challenor — a superb contralto and brilliant cook!

international soprano Pauline Tinsley. Vilna Challenor was a beautiful knitter and made me many pullovers, waistcoats, jumpers and cardigans. Everybody fancies them even today, 25 years after they were knitted. When my mother died in December 1986, Vilna and Raymond were very kind. Every Saturday she would telephone and say: "Come up to supper, I've made cawl," or "I've made cawl pys (pea soup)," or "I've made a pie, or I've made rissoles." I would then go up, have a lovely meal with Vilna and Raymond before she would fill a carrier bag with a home-made cake, sponge, Welsh cakes or macaroons — there would be something different every time. This lasted for five months because Vilna herself died suddenly in May 1987, just five months after my mother. I felt not only that I had lost one of my greatest artists but also one of my very best friends.

Vilna loved the Llanelli Young Music Lovers' Association and was thrilled to be the President's wife. It was at her request that we organised an annual carol festival. She loved carols and Christmas music and always sat with the readers and soloists in the Set Fawr or Big Seat. She loved opera and always accompanied Strade School on trips to see one. Her untimely death was mourned all over Llanelli. As a headmaster's wife she was loved and adored by staff and pupils alike. In the funeral service at the English Congregational Church, Burry Port, I sat next to Doug, the caretaker of Bryngwyn School. When he saw the coffin leave the church he said: "Gethin, the person lying in that coffin was a Christian lady. I was a widower for four years until I remarried and during that time Vilna Challenor insisted that I went there to lunch every day — and I was just the school caretaker. She had a heart of gold." He was right Vilna Challenor had a heart of pure gold.

Arthur Davies who achieved an amazing 'double' while singing in America.

Saving The Day

Arthur Davies

Watching a production of L'elisir D'amore by the Welsh National Opera in Cardiff during 1971 a prediction was made that one of its young principals was destined to become world famous. It was the first time I had heard Arthur Davies sing and meeting him after his magnificent performance I was convinced that this would come true.

Arthur had just graduated from the opera chorus to sing the lead tenor role of Nemerino, which includes the famous aria Una Furtiva Lagrima. With me in the audience that night was a group of friends from Llanelli, including Margaret Edwards, a very good musician. It was she who, during the interval, shared her thoughts that the young tenor would go very far in the world of opera. How true her words were, for Arthur Davies is recognised the world over as one of the finest tenors.

In 1976 Arthur was invited to sing in Llanelli for the first time by the town's Young Music Lovers' Association. The concert was in Zion Chapel, and he was an instant success with the audience. That night he shared the pulpit with Elizabeth Bainbridge the Covent Garden mezzo-soprano and Michael Rippon, the renowned bass baritone. Also taking part was Llanelli Girls' Grammar School choir under the direction of Tydfil Enston and Anne-Marie Marks. Since that time in 1976, Arthur has performed in Llanelli on several more occasions, each time with huge success.

In April 1986 he sang at Capel Newydd with international soprano Pauline Tinsley, with one of Wales's greatest contraltos Lynne Richards, Tycroes and the Rhymney Silurian Choir. Two years later Arthur sang in the 18th anniversary concert of the Young Music Lovers' Association at Moriah Chapel. This time in the company of Marian Roberts, and Evan Lloyd from Aberaeron, Trimsaran Ladies Choir and Llandybie Male Voice Choir.

The packed chapel enjoyed Arthur's superb performances of four major operatic arias, two Welsh ballads, an aria from Verdi's Requiem, four duets and a verse in the finale, The Holy City. His excellent singing was marvellously supported by the other artists and choirs. His visit had been one of the highlights of a very busy schedule that day. Arthur had been rehearsing at Covent Garden from 9am to 1.30pm in readiness for singing the tenor lead in Madam Butterfly. He then dashed by car to Llanelli arriving in Moriah Chapel with just enough time for a short rehearsal, before going to the Mayor's parlour in the Town Hall for an official welcome by the Mayor and Mayoress, Councillor and Mrs W Mathonwy Jones. After the two and a half hour concert and a meal at the home of Dilys Williams, he drove through the night to his home in Reading because on the

Rev. T Arthur Pritchard and his delightful wife Eirwen.

Sunday he had a performance in the Royal Academy of Music in London, and a further rehearsal at 2pm. What an honour it was for us to be fitted into his tight schedule and sing — so beautifully — in Llanelli.

Arthur, who retired from opera at the age of 60, sang in all the world's major opera houses and was in constant demand. Many leading musicians believed he should even have gained a place in the Guinness Book of Records. This came after an amazing double achievement when Arthur was singing at the Metropolitan Opera House, New York, in Britten's Glorianna. Late on a Friday evening his telephone rang bringing a plea for help from the Metropolitan. Dennis O'Neil was to have sung on the Saturday evening in a performance of Verdi's Rigoletto, but he had just cancelled. The voice on the other end of the phone asked: "Would Arthur save the performance?" He had not sung the role for nearly two years and there was no time for rehearsal on the Saturday. But Arthur Davies did it, and the result was a tremendous success. At the end of the opera he was given a crate of wine by Lord Harewood, President of the English National Opera as a thank you for his efforts.

This wasn't the only time Arthur had stood in at the last minute for Dennis O'Neil. On another occasion he raced from his Newport, Gwent, home to take over from O'Neil when he was taken ill shortly before the final act in a performance of I Puritani at the New Theatre, Cardiff.

Wifely Wonder
Mrs Pritchard

When the Rev. T Arthur Pritchard moved to Llanelli in September, 1953 to take up his new appointment as minister of the town's Triniti Chapel it wasn't long before members of the congregation there realised that they had an unique minister's wife in their midst — Mrs Eirwen Pritchard.

A bubbly personality, filled with Christian charity and doctrine Mrs Pritchard was a devout woman who threw herself into the work of a minister's wife with zest and zeal — nothing was too much or too little for this remarkable woman. She was a brilliant chairperson, could lead most beautifully in prayer, and was a down-to-earth Sunday School teacher. The children all loved her, complete with her deep Blaenau Ffestiniog accent, and she in turn loved them. She was just as at home, scrubbing the vestry floor when needed, polishing the chapel, washing dishes, or waiting at tables, but whatever Mrs Pritchard did, she did it with perfection and never any half measures.

She was also very attentive as a hostess, down the years inviting hundreds of ministers and friends to stay at the Manse in Felinfoel Road and even inviting several of the members home for coffee and sandwiches after the evening service on Easter Sunday evening before the 8pm rehearsal at Capel Newydd — kindness and generosity in abundance. Her home was always open — a house full of welcome. She often presided for the Bryn-ar-y-Mor Ladies Choir's after-church monthly hymn singing services in many of Llanelli's chapels. She was a great favourite with the choir and they loved to hear her lead in public prayer.

When I taught in Old Road Primary School, Mrs Pritchard would often invite me to the Manse in Felinfoel Road for tea and supper. Her husband would join us, but between the meals he would retire to the study to read and prepare sermons. She and I were then left in the living room to have a long chat. I loved those visits, and the huge welcome I always received from both of them.

On one occasion the concert party had asked the Elders of Triniti Chapel for use of the vestry to arrange a surprise 65th birthday party for Mrs Jenny Thomas, on January 31. As Jenny was also the chapel caretaker, we had to send her to the chapel house after Thursday evening's fellowship, and then get the key from her husband, slip quietly back into the vestry and put the tables up. Two women, Mrs Prithcard and myself — needless to say, the one who worked hardest was Eirwen Pritchard. The surprise party was on the following night, a Friday, but when the day dawned it had snowed overnight. We carried on with our plans only to find that the water in the vestry had frozen. As a result we had to carry some in buckets from Chapel House. Who took the lead in this arduous chore? None other than our dear minister's wife Mrs Pritchard of course. That evening because of the heavy snow both she and her husband had to walk two miles in the snow from Triniti Chapel, New Dock Road, to their home in Felinfoel Road.

Eirwen was also aware of one of my great weaknesses — I love a plate of home-made tart. Whenever we were on a Sunday School trip or a pilgrimage, Mrs Pritchard would have made a small fruit tart and hand it to me quietly, when no one was looking. She was a superb cook and whenever there was a bereavement or illness, she would cook something.

On another occasion she was on the St David's Day committee helping to raise funds for the Royal National Eisteddfod in Llanelli in 1962. The committee had arranged eight different nightly activities and on the Saturday evening there was a Noson Lawen with BBC TV's Michael Aspel as a special guest. Michael was staying overnight in Llanelli with the Pritchards and he often said that he had never experienced such kindness or welcome than in their home. He enjoyed his stay very much and told me afterwards: "Gethin, it's home from home, the Rev. and Mrs Pritchard are such lovely people — proper Christians — and Mrs Pritchard is a superb cook."

There was more to his visit than that, however. When he arrived in Felinfoel Road, he realised in his rush to leave London on the Saturday morning he had forgotten to pack his pyjamas, so he was loaned a pair of Mr Pritchard's for that evening!

If Mrs Pritchard was unique as a minister's wife then the forceful preaching of her husband was something all of its own too. He was excellent in the pulpit and possessed great faith and sincerity. He loved to preach the gospel of his beloved Saviour, but like his Master was also a practical person. He was a qualified woodwork teacher in a secondary school, before he turned his attention to the ministry. He was a faithful pastor who diligently looked after his flock. Members of Triniti fondly remember his masterly sermons and outstanding bible classes as well as his genuine kindness to all who met and knew him.

Without a doubt Mr and Mrs Pritchard, who both passed away some years ago, were one of the best ministry teams that Triniti Chapel has ever had.

Clever Cousins
The Leyshon family

One of the most predominant and well-known surnames in the New Dock area for over a century was that of Leyshon. There were three brothers, William, Reuben and Daniel, and amazingly each had a family of seven children.

William Leyshon lived in Trinity Road and his children were called Rachel, Harriet, Emily, Miriam, Emlyn, Tydfil and Lucy. Reuben lived in Stanley Street and his children were Mary Jane, Gwilym, Alice, Ernest, Gertie, Lily and Sid. The third brother Daniel lived in New Dock Road and his offspring were Lizzie, Annie, Herbert, Edith, Leyshon, Maggie and Edgar. Three of these cousins left an indelible mark on my life and character. I will be eternally thankful for knowing them and will always remember them with love and affection. Annie married Johnny Vaughan and lived in the family home, 14 New Dock Road. Annie Vaughan became well-known as a beautiful soprano soloist. Her clear bell-like voice was much in demand, but her greatest contribution was to her chapel — Triniti. She was the lead soprano in the choir for many years and, under the direction of Tom Jones with his wife Mary Etta at the organ, the choir became famous for its handling of anthems and choruses from oratorios, and won second prize in the Treorchy National Eisteddfod in 1928.

Annie was a superb soloist, and her charm and sincerity was always conveyed in her performances of Cartref, Darlun Fy Mam, Bwthyn Bach To Gwellt, My Hero, Come To The Fair and Smiling Throu'. For five years she was a faithful member of my concert party and continued singing until she was 75 when she moved to Llansamlet to live with her daughter Sybil. Annie was also quite at home in lighter music such as the operettas, which Triniti Chapel performed in St David's Hall — Giant's Castle, Idle Ben and Holiday on the Sands.

While with my concert party she sang two lead parts in musicals which Meiriona J Rees had written, and I had musically arranged — Dame True-Blue in Once upon a Time and Mrs Kathy Wallace in Ahoy There, at the parish hall. Annie also loved the Penny Readings at Triniti Chapel. Her contribution was immense — duets with William Henry Peckham, John Griffiths and Sarah Annie Wanglund. I will always remember Tell Me Gentle Stranger, Madam Will You Walk and O Lovely Peace. She was, without doubt, one of my idols — a Christian lady, faithful in prayer meeting, Sunday School and all chapel gatherings. Annie was a versatile singer. On one occasion in a concert at Moriah Chapel, although a top soprano, she doubled up at the last moment and sang the contralto solo He Was Despised, from Handel's Messiah with such feeling and sincerity that it brought the congregation to tears. A month later in a variety concert she sang with

Annie Vaughan celebrates her 70th birthday flanked by Gethin Hughes, right, and John Griffiths. Alongside she is seen enjoying a day trip.

Meiriona J Rees, a comedy version of the song Gendarmes, dressed as two police ladies and produced roars of laughter from the audience.

Tydfil Leyshon meanwhile, was the daughter of William Leyshon. She married Hubert Morgan and they lived in the family home in Trinity Road. Tydfil trained as a teacher and started her career at Halfway Primary School, where she taught for about two years before moving to Felinfoel Primary School, where she remained for many years.
Tydfil was an excellent violinist, having gained her FCV violin diploma. As a young girl, she played the instrument in Dock Chapel Orchestra with two Triniti friends, Annie Jane Griffiths and Sarah Annie Wanglund, under the conductorship of David Harries, the butcher. Later she played with Elvet and Nancy Marks, and Florence Holloway in the grammar school orchestra under the direction of Frank Phillips. I remember him once saying: "Tyd is a superb violinist, a marvellous sight reader and timekeeper." She also played in an orchestra under the direction of Dr. Vaughan Thomas in his opera The Maid of Llyn-y-Fan."

Known affectionately to many in Triniti Chapel as Auntie Tyd, she was a

Lily Sims

Tydfil Morgan

Sunday school teacher and deputy organist for over 40 years. She played the piano for the prayer meeting and fellowship for 25 years, and gave me my first chance to play the piano in public. She was well-read and loved a good concert, opera or oratorio. Her service to music in Llanelli was immense. She entertained ministers of the gospel and artists at her home and her kindness and generosity was tremendous. She was treasurer of Pwyllgor Gwyl Ddewi and helped many charities with house-to-house collections and by selling flags, but I will always remember Auntie Tyd for her musicianship, companionship and friendship — we played very many violin and piano duets — and above all for her sincerity.

The third of the Leyshon cousins to have had an influence on my life was Lily who married Charles Sims and lived in the Stanley Street house. She was another terrific character as was her husband Charles. Both were well-loved in the New Dock area. Lily nursed me as a baby — the traditional Welsh way in a large shawl wrapped tightly around us both — and sang an equally traditional hymn to send me to sleep. The tune was Dwyfor and the words, imprinted on my mind, were Iesu, Iesu, rwyt ti'n ddigon.

Around 40 years later when Maidie Bevan was President of the Women's Free Church Council, I was asked to conduct a Welsh singing festival at Capel Newydd. In front of me in the congregation singing her heart out was Auntie Lil, her beaming face a treat for anyone to see. I asked her if she would sing as a solo the same hymn she sang to me as a baby. She stood on her feet and to the accompaniment of Ella Williams on the organ, this 85-year-old lady sang it most beautifully.

Charles and Lily Sims were very religious people — converts of the 1904 Revival — but they also had a wonderful sense of humour. Lil had an infectious laugh and took her raincoat and umbrella everywhere even in the hot weather. She loved opera and once when a group of us had gone to the New Theatre, Cardiff, to hear and see Pauline Tinsley singing the role of Lady Macbeth we visited the star in her dressing room. Lil turned up as usual with her raincoat and umbrella and told Pauline: "My dear, you have worked hard tonight, I have brought you some sweets and a pot of home made Welsh honey for your throat."

She really was a determined character. One Saturday evening as she was papering her living room walls, she fell from a table and broke her arm. She thought it was too late to call a doctor and, determined not to miss Sunday service, embarked on her own brand of first aid using a wooden soup spoon, for a splint and a hastily made sling for her arm. It was Triniti Chapel as usual on Sunday, then on Monday morning she went to the local hospital outpatients' department, informing the doctor: "I broke my arm on Saturday night." What a brave and determined character. Lily won a certificate for over 80 years faithful Sunday School attendance. She was even present in Triniti Chapel the Sunday before she died, aged 85.

Adelaide Hall — one of the original Harlem jazz singers.

All That Jazz

Adelaide Hall

Born in New York and one of the original Harlem jazz singers the legendary Adelaide Hall brought all her character and charisma with her when she visited Llanelli on December 16, 1979. She was the celebrity guest in the Festival of Carols and Christmas Music at Zion Chapel organised by Llanelli Young Music Lovers' Association. In the early 1920s she appeared in revues and musicals such as Shuffle Along Blackbirds, Chocolate Kiddies and Showboat. She sang with greats such as Duke Ellington, Humphrey Lyttleton, Count Basie and Louis Armstrong and in 1927, made her classic recording of The Creole Love Call and Blues I Love to Sing. Another song she made famous was Bye-Bye Blackbird.

In 1931 Adelaide topped the bill at the London Palladium and performed in cabaret in Paris, London and New York. She worked with many of show business legends — Laurel and Hardy, Vera Lynn, Arthur Askey, Tessie O'Shea, Flanagan and Allen, Gracie Fields, George Formby and many others. In the 1950s she starred as Hattie in the London production of Kiss Me Kate.

The singer had made one previous visit to Llanelli — she appeared in the Astoria Theatre, New Dock Road, for a week in variety when it was owned by Dorothy Squires and Billy Reid. On this occasion however it was my role to meet her at the station on that December day in 1979 and when she stepped off the train, she looked like any other ordinary person. But believe me Adelaide Hall was anything but that.

From the station we headed for Zion Chapel where we rehearsed together. I was playing the organ for her while she sang White Christmas, Holy City and a selection of Negro spirituals. Mam sat in the chapel listening to Adelaide and myself. Later she told our minister the Rev. Gareth Davies: "When Adelaide Hall sang 'Were You There?' I felt cold shivers running down my spine and I felt as if Jesus Christ had touched me, her singing was so pure and sincere."

After the rehearsal, refreshments were served in the schoolroom by Mattie Bateman-Morris organist of St Alban's and Sybil Perrot, organist of Siloah Chapel. Later that evening, this very ordinary woman whom I met at the station and shared a snack with reappeared before us in an exquisite gold, evening gown and mesmerised the audience with her beautiful singing — every inch the star that she was. During her visit she stayed at the home of Keri and Enid Rosser of Denham Avenue and according to Keri, they were up until 3am listening to, and enjoying, her many anecdotes. After the festival, a group of us were invited to the home of Dr. and Mrs Graham Hodges in Felinfoel Road for a dinner party. Seated around the oval dining table with our host and hostess were Adelaide Hall, myself, Keri and Enid Rosser, Lyn Clement, headmaster of Coedcae Comprehensive School and his wife Ann, Mrs Megan Rees and Mrs Dorothy Nicholas. Afterwards Adelaide entertained us with Bye, Bye Blackbird and The Streets of London.

I later visited Adelaide at her London home and once shared lunch with her in the Savoy Hotel. She was a legend in her time, a fantastic jazz and blues singer and, of course, an expert on her native Negro spirituals. Everyone who was privileged to meet her will undoubtedly say that Adelaide Hall was also a Christian lady.

Adelaide, who died in 1993, was singing in concerts and theatres well into her eighties including prestigious venues such as the Royal Albert Hall, London, Queen Elizabeth Hall and Dublin Opera House. She often recalled, in telephone conversations afterwards, the bara brith she had for tea at Zion Chapel, beautifully baked by former Llanelli Borough Mayoress Enid Jones.

Hit For Six
Margaret Edwards

With famous Test Match cricket umpire Dai Davies as her father it is perhaps not surprising that Margaret Edwards met and became friends with a string of leading cricketers like Don Bradman, Len Hutton, Denis Compton and Bill Edrich along with people like that master of horror films, actor Boris Karloff.

Margaret spent her childhood in Stafford Street, Llanelli, before moving with her parents to Spowart Avenue. She trained as a teacher and worked for three years in Gravesend, before returning to Llanelli to teach in Market Street, Ysgol Dewi Sant, Halfway — where I taught with her — and finally Pembrey primary schools.

In her younger days Margaret Edwards was like a Parisian model, very pretty, charming and intelligent, with exquisite taste in clothes. After returning to Llanelli she met and married John Edwards then head of the history department at Ysgol y Strade and later author of several fascinating books. She was an excellent musician, a beautiful accompanist and on some occasions deputised at the organ of Dock Chapel.

For many years before her death Margaret was confined to a wheelchair through illness, but her courage, grit and determination in the face of adversity can be seen as a lesson to us all. With her husband John she still managed to attend orchestral concerts and her love of music was clearly displayed by her long and loyal support to Llanelli Young Music Lovers' Association.

Margaret Edwards — in her younger days she was like a Parisian model.

Frank Herbert with his wife Betty and, left, his brother James. For three years both brothers sang with the Gethin Hughes Concert Party.

Dockland Duo
Frank and James Herbert

Arthur and Sarah Ann Herbert of Stanley Road, New Dock, Llanelli had a large family — 10 children in all. The eldest were four girls — Irene, Maggie, Carrie and Myra — followed by six boys — Frank, John, Elwyn, James, Hywel and Syd. All had good singing voices, but Frank and James were outstanding, both becoming soloists — Frank a baritone, James, a tenor.

Frank as the eldest boy followed his father Arthur in more ways than one, in business as a coal merchant eventually taking over from his father, and also as a conductor. Arthur used to lead the singing in the week-night services at Triniti Presbyterian Chapel where Frank was choirmaster for 42 years. James — Jim to his friends — like the remaining brothers went into the armed forces.

Frank received voice training with the renowned David Brazell from Pwll, and his voice remained remarkable even into his late 70s when he was still singing in concerts and services and was a member of Cor Cydweli. In 1937 he was a member of Llanelli Choral Society when, under the baton of Edgar Thomas it won first prize at the Fishguard Royal National Eisteddfod. He lived in Pwll with his wife Betty in Maes yr Haf and was an elder in Triniti Chapel following in the footsteps of his father, grandfather and great grandfather. James his brother had a beautiful tenor voice, one of the best I have ever heard, but unfortunately he did not have any voice training.

For three years both Frank and Jim were members of my concert party. During that time they delighted many an audience with duets such as Larboard Watch and Lle Treigla'r Caferi. They sang these with perfect harmony and sweet blend — a sound that will live in my memory as long as I live.

Jim had an infectious smile, a wicked gleam in his eye, a healthy laugh and, above all, a kind personality. Sadly, he died in May 1977 at the age of 54. Among my many fond memories of him is the fact that he was the first person for me to accompany in public at a welcome home concert for servicemen returning to the town after the Second World War. Jim sang some of the Neapolitan songs he had learned during the war in Naples — Santa Lucia and O Sole O Mio — as well as Nirvana and the famous Welsh solo Yr Hen Gerddor — he was superb.

I was not the only one to be entranced by his fine voice. One member of Triniti's congregation, Gladys Spencer, told me: "If I was a rich woman I would pay for James

Edna Bonnell and, alongside, her popular Welsh language publication Weithiau'n Deg.

Herbert go to the Royal Academy for singing lessons." In later years Frank, who died in December 2002, sang with a number of accomplished personalities. Lle Treigla'r Caferi was tackled alongside famous Welsh tenor Richie Thomas in a concert at Greenfield Chapel. He also sang this on a number of occasions with Trimsaran tenor Hugh Davies. In 1992 he sang a duet with two Blue Riband winners — contralto Lavina Thomas and soprano Marion Roberts. As organist I worked regularly with him when he was choirmaster and it was an enjoyable partnership

Jim's wife Jean died some years ago and Noela, his daughter together with Eirlys, Frank's daughter and Betty, Frank's widow, are faithful members of Triniti Chapel. I shall always remember the happy times, including rehearsals, I had when playing for Frank and James Herbert — duettists supreme.

Dramatic entry
Edna Bonnell

The first time I heard the name of Edna Bonnell was in 1941 when my mother, herself a very good amateur actress, took me to Ebenezer vestry to see Tom Griffiths's drama company perform the Welsh comedy Bili. This was a hilarious Welsh comedy about a schoolboy played by the ageing Tom Griffiths in short trousers, blazer and school cap, with Edna Bonnell as his mother.

Also in the cast was another well known veteran Llanelli actor, Ivor Evans, whose daughter, Mary Rees taught in Lakefield Primary School. Both Tom Griffiths and Ivor Evans had worked on the Llanelli Mercury newspaper before running their own printing business. Edna Bonnell, Tom Griffiths and Ivor Evans were an excellent team and kept the audience in stitches.

In the comedy Bili's mother would ask him to play a tune on the violin, and he would inquire: "Home Sweet Home, Mam?" for that was the only piece he could play. Another popular Welsh drama that these three marvellous performers acted in was Mrs Biddles by Eddie Parry, a well known Llanelli musician and dramatist. Both these comedies played to packed audiences throughout Wales.

Edna Nicholas was a native of Llwynhendy and a regular worshipper at the village's Nazareth chapel, before moving to Libanus, Pwll when she married Brinley Bonnell, the youngest of 11 children of the Bonnell family. Two of his brothers became well known, Tom as a popular baritone and Alderman Robert Bonnell as a Mayor of Llanelli and headmaster of Park Street Primary School. Brin's sister Maggie, who later became Mrs Maggie Trueman, was a soprano soloist in much demand throughout Wales. His other brothers and sister were Mary, William, David, Evan, John, Joseph and Stanley, who died last year at the age of 91. Stan possessed a lovely baritone voice and on his 90th birthday sang Y Marchog — an outstanding achievement. His daughter, Menna, is one of the organists at Libanus Chapel.

Brin and Stan were very close, being the two youngest of the family and were very good bowls players. So when Edna married Brin, she joined a well known and talented family. Soon however, Edna became equally well known, and eventually became the shining star of the family.

There were a number of Welsh drama companies in Llanelli in the past. They included that of May Bevan Smedley and her husband Dick; Lizzie Moss Lloyd and her company which included Betty Williams and Ena Edwards; James Edwards and his company which featured Margretta Every and David Thomas. But the most popular of these entertainment group's was Pwll Drama Company produced and directed by Edna Bonnell. Edna's actors included Megan Rees, Brenda Davies, Martin Griffiths, Hugh Barney and of course her neighbour, life-long friend and fellow member of Libanus, Pwll — Edwina Barney. Her beloved Brin was one of the star turns, who had the talent and charisma of Charlie Chaplin. Edna knew she had only to put Brin on stage and he would bring the house down.

Edna wrote most of her Welsh plays for her own players. She knew her cast and wove the characters around them. Edna wrote seven full length Welsh plays, three of which have been published: Awyr yr awr Olaf; Man gwyn Man Draw; Y Garreg Rhwystr; Chwildro; Rhoi Pethau'n Iawn; Emyr Caradog and Wncwl Titus. They have been performed across Wales and for some years appeared annually at the London Welsh Club. They were staged in small village halls, chapel vestries, indeed anywhere there was a platform and curtains. Edna once related a story of days when they were performing in the heart of the country. It was the fashion then to have a chairman, usually a wealthy farmer. On this occasion, the chairman had given his speech and sat in the centre of the stage. Edna and her company had to perform the first act of the play around him. Fortunately during the interval, he decided to move and sit in the audience.

Sadly, the talents of this great Welsh lady were not recognised in Wales for she was a tremendous actress, an excellent producer and a brilliant author. Brin died in 1987, three weeks before their Diamond Wedding. They were a devoted and talented couple. One must admire the courage and bravery of Edna, who carried on entertaining people long after her husband's death. She and her close friend Edwina Barney, whose husband Hugh died around 18 years previously, continued to act and take part in the Libanus Party, giving programmes to chapels and various societies, for many years after.

Edna did a great deal of radio work in the 1940s and 1950s. She performed with singers such as Llangennech soprano, Elizabeth Evans; Ifor Rees and Dafydd Evans and also in Welsh Rarebit with Mai Jones. Edna and Brin took part with a special company in Under Milk Wood, giving performances in Laugharne, on BBC TV and in Holland. Edna's part throughout was Mrs Dai Bread One. She even published a succesful full length Welsh novel — Weithiau'n Deg (Sometimes Fair) — which enjoyed a good response. Edna was a great friend of my mother's and wrote some lovely Welsh verses to celebrate her 80th birthday.

Edna and Brin were the caretakers of Ysgol y Strade and lived in School House. I spent many happy hours in their company. In 1962, when the National Eistedfod was held in Llanelli, Strade school was used as a hostel. I was one of the wardens and slept there throughout the week. Every evening between 11pm and 12.30am Edna and Brin would invite me in to their home for a snack. In 1965 I was appointed music master at Ysgol y Strade and often found myself a guest of the school caretakers. When Edna and Brin retired to live in Bassett Terrace, Pwll, I was often invited to their home there.

As well as her great talents as novelist, actress and dramatist, Edna was also a superb cook and a grand host. I have enjoyed many meals in her home and for years I would call there on Christmas Eve for a ritual lunch of salmon or sausage and chips, followed by home-made mince pies or Christmas cake. Next door to Edna and Brin lived their life-long friends Hugh and Edwina Barney. For many years, Edna, Edwina, Brin and myself sat around the table and I enjoyed every moment of their company. So natural were these three giants of Welsh Drama that I felt as though I was on the stage in their midst. I laughed a lot around that table and my annual visit to Edna's became the highlight of the Christmas holidays.

One of the greatest compliments to Edna — who died, aged 90, in 1997 — was given by Mr Glyn Hughes, former Head of the Welsh department at Llanelli Boys' Grammar School. He was taking us in Advanced Welsh in Form VI back in 1954 and the topic was Welsh Drama. Glyn Hughes had spoken of Saunders Lewis and many other Welsh dramatists when suddenly he mentioned Edna Bonnell. We boys laughed. Very seriously, Glyn Hughes replied: "Don't laugh boys. Edna Bonnell is very much underestimated in Wales. She has contributed greatly to Welsh Drama and is without doubt a very talented person."

Mary Glangwendraeth who collected many awards for her singing prowess.

Trademark Tune

Mary Glangwendraeth

The song Smiling Throu' became the trademark of Trimsaran's Mary Glangwendraeth. The popular concert party member's real name was Mary Williams and she was the eldest daughter of a couple who lived near Trimsaran. Her father was known as Billy'r Bwtchwr and the family were all staunch members of Llandyri Church.

Her only brother, William John, a fine baritone and National Eisteddfod winner, was choirmaster at Sardis Independent Chapel and his daughters were the well known sisters Peggy and Anita Williams. Both were also National winners, with Peggy a double Blue Riband winner. Mary's sister Letitia was well known throughout Britain as a contralto. Mary took her stage name Glangwendraeth from Glangwendraeth Farm, Kidwelly, where she worked as a farm hand. She married David Roger Williams, who was organist and choirmaster at St. Illtyd's Church, Pembrey for 50 years, a role taken by his father for 50 years before him. They made their home in Parc y Medws, near Rock House and Pembrey Farm on Pembrey Mountain.

Mary was a terrific soprano soloist, having won in the National Eisteddfod and collected many awards in other competitions. Her popular solos were Llam y Cariadau; Ysbryd y Mynydd; Ocean Thou Mighty Monster and The Jewel Song from Faust. However, it was a simple ballad that ensured her popularity — Smiling Throu'. She was a member of my concert party for 21 years and was always asked to sing this which she made her own, with a brilliant top 'A' note at the end. She could do this until just three months before she died at the age of 87, a truly remarkable feat.

On one occasion, a coachload of us from Llanelli travelled to the New Theatre, Cardiff to see Don Carlos with the Welsh National Opera Company. The part of Princess Eboli was sung by the international mezzo-soprano Janet Coster, who had invited us to her dressing room after the performance. Everybody including Mary wanted Janet's autograph and then one of our group informed Miss Coster that Mary Williams could also sing. Janet's immediate response was "Sing for me, my dear." Mary turned to me and asked what she should sing. I replied: "Smiling Throu' of course." She sang it superbly in the confines of that dressing room.

Janet Coster was so thrilled at hearing this impromptu performance that she asked Mary to autograph her score of Don Carlos and added: "If I'll be able to sing like that at the age of 70 let alone 85, I shall be a proud woman." Another time the international soprano Rita Hunter was singing with us in our 25th anniversary concert at Moriah

Gethin gyda
Gwyndaf Ryan
Jon.

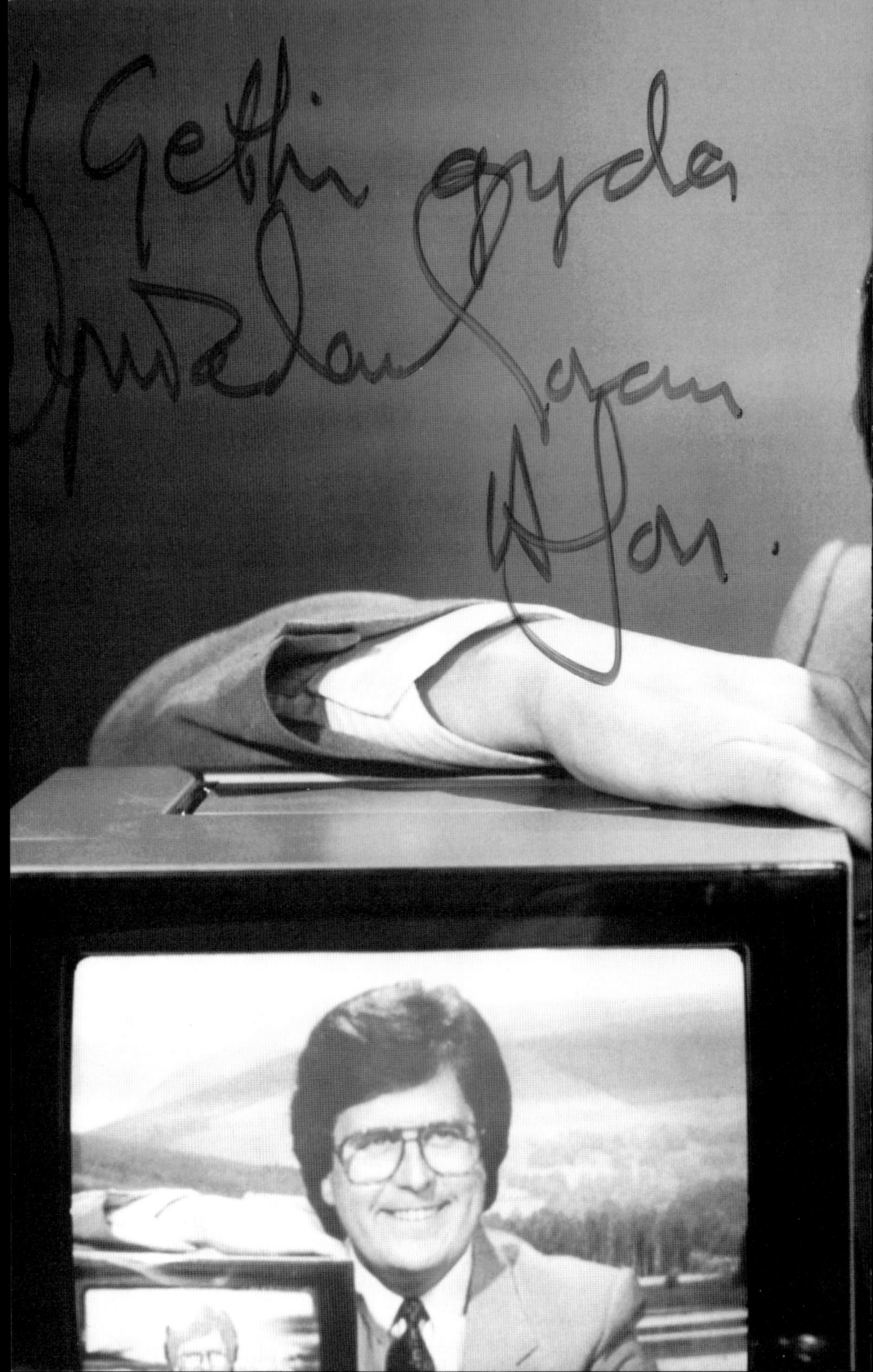

Arfon Haines-Davies — ever popular as a TV presenter and also with his Llanelli audience.

Daphne Edwards   **Joy Davies**

Chapel. Rita insisted on doing an item with the girls of the concert party. I composed an arrangement of My Hero for Rita and 'the girls' — Vera Tiley-James, Vilna Challenor, Daphne Edwards, Joy Davies, Betty Tovey and last but not least Mary Williams. As they sang in the pulpit of Moriah Chapel, Vera Tiley-James stood on one side of Rita Hunter, and Mary on the other, Mary was rather a big woman, but small at the side of the 21 stone international soprano. At the end of the song Rita caught hold of Mary and Vera and squeezed them until they were "like a pancake." Mary commented that she thought she was being flattened.

Later when being interviewed by Garry Nicholas on Swansea Sound she said that my concert party had given her a new lease of life after the death of her husband as had Triniti Chapel, where she became a member. Garry ended the interview by asking her to sing the song that everybody associated with her — Smiling Throu' which as ever she obligingly did.

Father's Footsteps

Arfon Haines-Davies

The first time I met Arfon Haines-Davies was in December 1985 at Moriah Chapel, when he was special guest at the Festival of Carols and Christmas Music organised by Llanelli Young Music Lovers' Association. He enthralled everybody with his inspired and masterly dramatic readings. Afterwards in the vestry, a meal had been arranged, and seated at the table were some of the vice-presidents — Yvonne Watkin-Rees; Garry Nicholas, Iwan Rees, Mair Jones, Mavis Williams, Rev. Dewi Davies and the guest soloist Janice Davies-Rees; Mr and Mrs Dai Smith; Betty Tovey and my mother, Blod.

As we chatted over our meal we discovered that Arfon was not only a dynamic, charming person, with loads of charisma, but also possessed a generous and kind heart. He refused any financial expenses from the young musicians, and his adamant answer to me was: "Not on any account. I won't accept a penny. It's been my great pleasure to meet the young people and it was worth coming down all the way from Cardiff to hear you play the Moriah organ so superbly."

On hearing this Rev. Dewi Davies, minister of Moriah stood up on behalf of the association and commented: "Knowing his father so well I could only expect that from his son." Who was Arfon's father? The Rev. J Haines-Davies, of Colwyn Bay — joint secretary with Rev. Dewi Davies of Sunday School Gee Medals of Wales. Arfon was born in Caernarfon where his father was a Wesleyan minister. After studying to be a teacher in Trinity College, Carmarthen, he taught for a few years in Treffynnon, North Wales, and then studied in the Central College of Speech and Drama in London. For many years he has been one of the most familiar faces on HTV as a presenter.

Later he revisited the Llanelli Young Music Lovers' Association to give a talk. Once again the young people enjoyed his company and our friendship was rekindled. He visited my home in Hick Street for a meal and commented what a good cook I was. He invited me to Cardiff and gave me a tour of the HTV studios before driving me to his beautiful home in Cyncoed.

While I was there I saw his collection of china mugs — faces of famous personalities like Charlie Chaplin; Laurel and Hardy; The Marx Brothers; Maurice Chevalier and many others. He also had pre-war posters of such famous music-hall personalities as Gracie Fields, George Formby, Nellie Wallace and Max Miller. Also around the house and in its garage, it was apparent that Arfon is a great railway enthusiast — having collected railwayana of all kinds from all over Britain.

Marian Roberts, left, seen here with Anne Ziegler.

Nightingale Notes
Marian Roberts

Llanelli concert-goers loved the Anglesey nightingale Marian Roberts who lived with her husband Jack on a large sheep farm in Brynsiencyn. Plas Trefarthen, a lovely mansion, which Marion had converted into a three star hotel offering home cooking. Situated on the shores of the Menai Straits overlooking Snowdonia and Caernarvon Castle, it was a true paradise for tourists. Talented Marian is a National Eisteddfod winner, many times over in the open soprano competition, and in the 1978 National at Cardiff, won the coveted Blue Riband.

Marian sang on three occasions with Llanelli Young Music Lovers' Association — in Triniti, Moriah and Greenfield Chapels. In October 1988 she sang with Arthur Davies, the world famous tenor and Evan Lloyd, the well-known Welsh bass to a capacity audience at Moriah Chapel. On that occasion Arthur Davies specially requested to sing Hywel a Blodwen with her and his words to me afterwards were: "Gethin, what a joy and pleasure to sing with Marian Roberts. Such a beautiful voice, superb musician and an exquisite artiste."

The Anglesey Nightingale — Blue Riband winner Marian Roberts.

Marian has very many friends who are fans of hers in Llanelli and for a number of years in October a group of 20 of us travelled up to stay with her and Jack in her home and hotel, Plas Trefarthen. Each time we enjoyed to the full the excellent food, the delightful surroundings, and the lovely concerts Marian and some of her friends gave after our evening meal. The couple have since moved into a new home — Bodlawen — in Brynsiencyn overlooking Caernarvon Castle. Marian is a sweet and kind soul, one of Wales' finest soloists, who is also the organist of her chapel. A few years ago she sang in the St David's Day Festival in the Royal Albert Hall. Friends of mine, Gwen and Roydon Rees, who keep the Ridgemount Hotel in Gower Street, said after hearing her on that occasion many of those present thought her one of the best soloists the festival had seen for many years.

Edwina Barney and, inset, Sybil Perrott who both contributed immensely to Llanelli's rich music scene.

Shining Lights
Sybil and Edwina

Among female personalities who have contributed to Llanelli's lively music and drama scene down the years and also provided invaluable support to Llanelli Young Music Lovers' Association are Sybil Perrott and Edwina Barney.

Edwina, from Pwll attended the village's primary school, and later Stradey Central School. One of her early fellow vocalists was the entertainer Dorothy Squires from Dafen. Edwina's mother was the organist of Libanus Chapel, Pwll, for many years, and Edwina and her sister Meriel both took an active part in all chapel services in Libanus. Edwina has taken a leading role in dramatic societies and performances all her life, ever since her days at Stradey School. She also has a lovely voice and has sung in many of the operettas with Eddie Parry in Stradey School.

Edwina and her late husband Hugh Barney were for 40 years members of Edna Bonnell's famous Welsh Drama Company, and acted with Edna and Brin all over Wales. Two of her best known, though contrasting roles were as Cordelia Harries in Na Fernwch and Queenie in Emyr Caradog, while another was as a land girl in the wartime comedy Y Garreg Rhwystr. She also performed on more than one occasion in the Laugharne Festival in Dylan Thomas's Under Milk Wood. She was also the first to play the role of Lady McDuff in a Welsh Shakespeare production. Edwina and Hugh acted in five productions with Cwmni Drama Cymraeg, Llanelli, directed by Garry Nicholas. She will always be remembered for her excellent performance with Llanelli Amateur Operatic Society in The Arcadians. As a vice-president of Llanelli Music Lovers' Association Edwina gave an invaluable contribution to its existence. She has given excellent readings in its carol festivals, taken part in many panel games and helped in our Christmas parties.

Sybil Perrott was another from Llanelli whose musical talents shone brightly. Her father Sam was a lecturer in the town's technical college and for many years an elder and Sunday School teacher in Capel Newydd. Sybil became deputy organist to Mr Robert Charles, and accompanied performances of Mozart's 12th Mass and Mendelsohn's Hymn of Praise at the chapel with Elsie Suddaby, Gwen Catley, David Lloyd and Webster Booth. In 1939, she went to Manchester College of Music and studied there for three years, gaining her LRAM. Sybil was an excellent accompanist and organist, roles she occupied for many years with Côr Glandulais. After her retirement from that role Sybil taught the piano. For many years she was organist at Siloah Congregational Chapel, and for a period accompanist of Kidwelly Choral Society. Sadly, Sybil died in February 2002.

Sheila Lochead — Prime Minister's daughter and a fascinating speaker.

First Lady
Sheila Lochead

Without a doubt, one of the most interesting, intelligent and charming people I have ever met is Sheila Lochead of Langland Road, Mumbles, the youngest of the six children of the Rt. Hon. and Mrs Ramsey MacDonald. Sheila's mother died when she was just a year old but her father became the first Labour Prime Minister of Britain in 1924. On that occasion he remained in power for only 10 months, but his second term of office lasted for six years from 1929 to 1935, the first two being as head of a Labour government and the remaining four years from 1931, a National government.

Sheila and her sister Joan shared the duties of hostess at 10 Downing Street, until Joan went to college to study medicine. This left Sheila, at a very early age, to become the lady of No 10, but despite this she soon proved that she was an excellent hostess and her father was very proud of her. Sheila recalled that one person who showed great kindness and friendship to her in those early years was Mrs Stanley Baldwin, wife of the former Prime Minister. Mrs Baldwin advised her on curtains, decor and several other household matters in No 10.

The red-carpeted corridor behind the famous black No. 10 door that TV has these days made so familiar leads to the Cabinet Room and the office of the secretaries and clerks. This corridor it seems was a favourite place for Sheila and Joan to practice their golf. On the first floor of 10 Downing Street is the official reception room, dining room and two big drawing rooms that are used for official banquets and dinner parties. The second floor, which later became a self-contained flat, housed the private rooms of the Prime Minister and his family. Later, Sheila married Andrew Lochead and they had three children.

Sheila Lochead was another of those fascinating people I first met when she attended one of the Llanelli Young Music Lovers' Association's carol festival's as a special guest, this time in December 1987. She chose some very interesting Christmas material to read and recite and was such a success that the youngsters immediately asked her back to one of the association's fortnightly meetings at Moriah vestry. This she readily did 18 months later when she gave a talk based on her very interesting life.

On a later occasion I was invited by Paul Williams, head of the sixth form at Coedcae Comprehensive School to accompany him on a visit to her home at Langland Road, Mumbles. Over afternoon tea in front of a log fire the three of us again chatted about aspects of her interesting life. She told us of how as a schoolgirl she travelled on the bus from Whitehall every day to the Collegiate School in North London — no taxi or a chauffeur driven car just plain service bus. She also recalled how, during her time at 10 Downing Street, she met a galaxy of world famous personalities including Charlie Chaplin, Hungarian violinist Kreisler, who had come to play for the Prime Minister and friends and Paul Robeson the famous negro bass, who often visited and sung for them at No 10.

Early in 1935 Sheila was asked to represent the British Government in Germany and while there was entertained to tea by Hitler. She told us: "We chatted about everything including the German education system. I was so shocked because there was nothing outstanding or startling about this rather small figure. But that night at the Berlin Opera House in a rally to open the Winter Relief Campaign, Hitler was mesmeric, absolutely holding the vast audience of thousands spellbound. His performance was something that I had never experienced before or since."

In 1942 her brother Malcolm was appointed British High Commissioner in Canada and Sheila went with him as housekeeper. They became friends of the Canadian Prime Minister McKenzie King who like themselves was of Scottish origin. While in Canada Sheila entertained Jomo Kenyatta and many other distinguished people and worked with the Fighting French, the Free Dutch, the Polish Contingent and the British pilots.

She has fond memories of meeting the great Keir Hardie and still has a very loving place in her heart for her native Scotland especially Lossiemouth where her father was born. In 1926 Epstein sculpted a head and shoulder bust of her father Ramsey MacDonald which some years ago Sheila presented to the House of Commons.

Sharing some rare moments with Norma Procter in the garden of her home.

Rule Britannia
Norma Procter

Queen of contralto would be an apt way of describing Norma Procter, who has certainly made an impact on the music loving fraternity in Llanelli. Her first visit — to a Llanelli Young Music Lovers' Association concert was memorable to say the least. Regarded by many great musicians as the finest contralto since Kathleen Ferrier, Norma performed Rule Britannia so superbly that night at Moriah Chapel in 1982, she was begged to return two years later, in 1984, this time at Capel Newydd.

Norma Procter was born in Cleethorpes, Lincolnshire, but now lives in Grimsby. As a young girl she was a piping soprano, winning many competitive festivals but for four years she stopped singing to concentrate on academic studies. After this long vocal rest, Norma's voice turned into a deep contralto, with a two octave range and at 18 she started vocal studies with Roy Henderson one of the most famous voice trainers in Britain, who had previously mentored the legendary Kathleen Ferrier, .

Norma began her professional career at the age of 20 in the Glyndebourne Opera Chorus. She received musicianship lessons from Alec Redshaw and studied Lieder with Hans Oppenheim and Paul Hamburger. After making her London debut in Southwark Cathedral in 1948 she quickly followed in the footsteps of her great friend Kathleen Ferrier, soon becoming one of the world's most sought-after contraltos.

Highlights for Norma in an illustrious world-wide career were when she sang with Joan Sutherland at Brecon Cathedral in Peregolossi's Stabat Mater, and when she sang Rule Britannia at the Last Night of the Proms at the Royal Albert Hall under the baton of Sir Malcolm Sargent. Her recordings include Messiah, Elijah, Samson, Mahler's 2nd, 3rd and 8th symphonies Brahms/Mahler Lieder and also a selection of ballads.

Norma Procter possesses a genial, kind, warm-hearted personality, which I discovered on meeting her for the first time in April 1982. Her performance of He Was Despised during her second visit was a treasure to be remembered. The rich contralto voice, the depth of feeling and pathos, the sincere, personality all blending together to give us one of those rare musical moments. She also sang Spring, Lost Chord, Bless This House, Love's Old Sweet Song and O Peaceful England, from Merrie England.

Some years later I was privileged to meet Norma again, this time in Grimsby. I was staying with friends Robert and Ann Edwards in Horncastle. Robert used to sing in my concert party many years ago. He was present in the concert at Moriah Chapel in 1982,

Norma Procter, who followed in the footsteps of her idol, Kathleen Ferrier.

and when I suggested that we may be able to meet Norma, he was delighted. She gave us a terrific welcome and a visit which was meant to last an hour developed into one of nearly four. On that occasion she showed us one of her most treasured possessions — an autographed photograph of her heroine Kathleen Ferrier which read: "To Norma, all the best in the future — much love, Kathy." She is now semi-retired and concentrates on teaching and giving master classes.

Norma took over the role of Eurydice in Gluck's opera Orpheus from Kathleen when she died while it was being staged at Covent Garden Opera House in 1953.

In recent times I have been lucky enough to visit her again, in the company of Rev. Robert Parry of Wrexham. After listening to that glorious voice once more it would be wonderful to think that she would restart public singing.

Rocks Of Ages
Some wonderful pals

During my later life I have become indebted to a trio of wonderful pals — three solid rocks — people I can rely on through thick and thin — it is a joy to know them and a pleasure to be in their company. They are Meirion Rees, Eifion Thomas and Iwan Rees.

When Iwan joined the staff of Ysgol Y Strade in September 1983 we hit it off immediately. Soon he became a vice president of Llanelli Young Music Lovers' Association. Iwan is a good pianist and violinist, has a delightful tenor voice and although when we first met he was captain of Llanelli Wanderers rugby team, he was still a great opera lover and had a strong affection for Welsh hymns. Together we saw about five operas at Covent Garden and many more with the Welsh National Opera. We also had three lovely holidays in Majorca, Egypt and Russia. I also played the organ at his wedding to Margaret in 1985. When my mother died in 1986 Iwan was very supportive and I shall never forget his kindness. His mother Joan is a lovely lady and his father Dennis a gentleman — both active in Moriah chapel. I also played the organ at the weddings of his brother Alun and sister, Sian. Iwan is now headmaster of Ysgol Gyfun Maesyryrddfa and remains a good pal.

The second of these rocks is Meirion Rees, of Penyrheol Drive. Meirion was one of the organists at Adulam Baptist Chapel, Llanelli for many years and head of the geography department at Ysgol Gyfun Y Strade. Meirion often deputises for me at the organ of Triniti Chapel. I first met him as a young student teacher when he came to do teaching practice in Ysgol Y Strade in 1970. Then, we became close friends in 1981 when I commuted two days a week to Ysgol Gyfun Graig where Meirion was again head of geography. The friendship soon grew and he became one of my greatest pals.

Meirion took main parts with the Llanelli Operatic Society of which I became the musical director in 1983. These were in productions which included The Gondoliers and The Arcadians. Meirion also joined my concert party where he gave invaluable service for 14 years. During my recent illness he has been terrific, his friendship means a great deal to me as does that of his wife, Mary, and family. Meirion is a wonderful pal and like Iwan a solid support whom I can safely lean on at all times.

The third and last of my rocks is Eifion Thomas, musical director of Cor Meibion Llanelli. Eifion is one of Wales's most brilliant musicians — a good accompanist and organist, a very good conductor, accomplished composer and an excellent tenor soloist. I first met him when he was a fifth form pupil at Llanelli Boys' Grammar School where

Iwan Rees, with myself and my Danish friend Odile Scharbau on a day out in the Welsh countryside.

I taught for a year in 1960. Eifion was one of a male voice group in the school's prize day in Moriah Chapel. They were singing Llanfair arranged by Mansel Thomas, a piece which Cor Meibion now regularly sing. I next came into contact with him six years later in 1966 when he did his teaching practice in Ysgol Y Strade. We became friends, but our friendship really blossomed when I became accompanist to Cor Meibion Llanelli in January 1997 where he is musical director. Eifion has become a wonderful pal and a caring friend. He is so humble and endearing particularly when one acknowledges he has conducted the Thousand Voices at the Royal Albert Hall and performed as soloist at St David's Hall and the Royal Albert Hall. He was headmaster of Halfway County Primary school for 23 years and master of the eisteddfod choir in Llanelli in 2000. An added bonus to his friendship is that of his wife Susanne and daughter Sophie.

But if the three lads mentioned here could be considered my best pals then I could not let my thoughts on the value of friendship pass without mention of a few others whose long time companionship has made my life altogether richer. Teifryn Rees in particular must figure high up the list. I have accompanied this tenor soloist on many occasions since 1965. Our performances together have taken us throughout England and Wales and have included a memorable tour of Ireland during which we played at the prestigous Dublin Concert Hall and Kilkenny Cathedral. We have also teamed up for TV performances and at masonic functions where Teifryn holds a high office. Our paths also cross annually at the National Eisteddfod as we are both members of the Gorsedd. Teifryn is as at home singing before a handful of listeners as a crowded auditorium and always keen to offer support where he can. Away from the musical arena he and his wife Olive have seldom been far away when I have needed help or assistance and are true friends.

Margaret Skinner is another. She and her family have been friends of mine for more than 60 years. Margaret was a very successful Town Mayoress in 2002-3 when her son Edward was Town Mayor. She

Eifion Thomas.

has been an elder in Triniti Chapel since 1984, President of Llanelli Free Church Council and also of the Presbyterian Local Ladies Association. Also a long term family friend has been one of Triniti's most faithful and long-serving members, Margaret Williams who played the piano in the Sunday School and Band of Hope. She is now 91 and as close a friend as ever.

Bill Williams, who was headmaster of Stebonheath School for some years and his wife Eirwen who taught in Llanelli Primary school are two others I hold close to my heart as is Megan Rees, a member of Capel Als who down the years certainly made her mark on eisteddfodau throughout the Principality — even carrying the Horn of Plenty in the 1962 Llanelli National proclamation ceremony. Both she and her family have made their mark on my life.

Sweet soprano-voiced Betty Jenkins, a member of my concert party for more than six years and also a faithful member of Triniti Chapel for many years is another I count close. Betty together with James Herbert was the first person I played the piano for. It was at the Welcome Home tea in Triniti vestry in 1945 for servicemen returning from the Second World War

Among my dearest friends has been Susan Tiplady, a fellow teacher on the staff of Ysgol Y Strade for 20 years during which time we enjoyed a variety of school trips. She was a vice-president of Llanelli Young Music Lovers' Asociation for 15 years and is currently a deacon at Bethel Baptist Chapel. Both Susan and husband Robert are wonderful friends and have always been a pleasure and delight to know.

Margaret Skinner.

Finally there is Dai and Einir Smith. Einir was my deputy organist in Triniti for many years and Dai a fellow elder for 21 years. We taught together for a time at Llanelli Boys' Grammar School. Dai was one of four founder vice-presidents of the Llanelli Young Music Lovers' Association and maintained his links for 25 years. All of these people I would consider the salt of the earth. They have always welcomed me into their lives and homes and I in turn have always enjoyed their companionship.

Meirion Rees.

Some of the members of Llanelli Young Music Lovers' Association with its president Raymond Challenor; chairman Gethin Hughes and four vice-presidents – Dai Smith, Rev. Dewi Davies, Enid Mathonwy-Jones and Mattie Bateman-Morris.

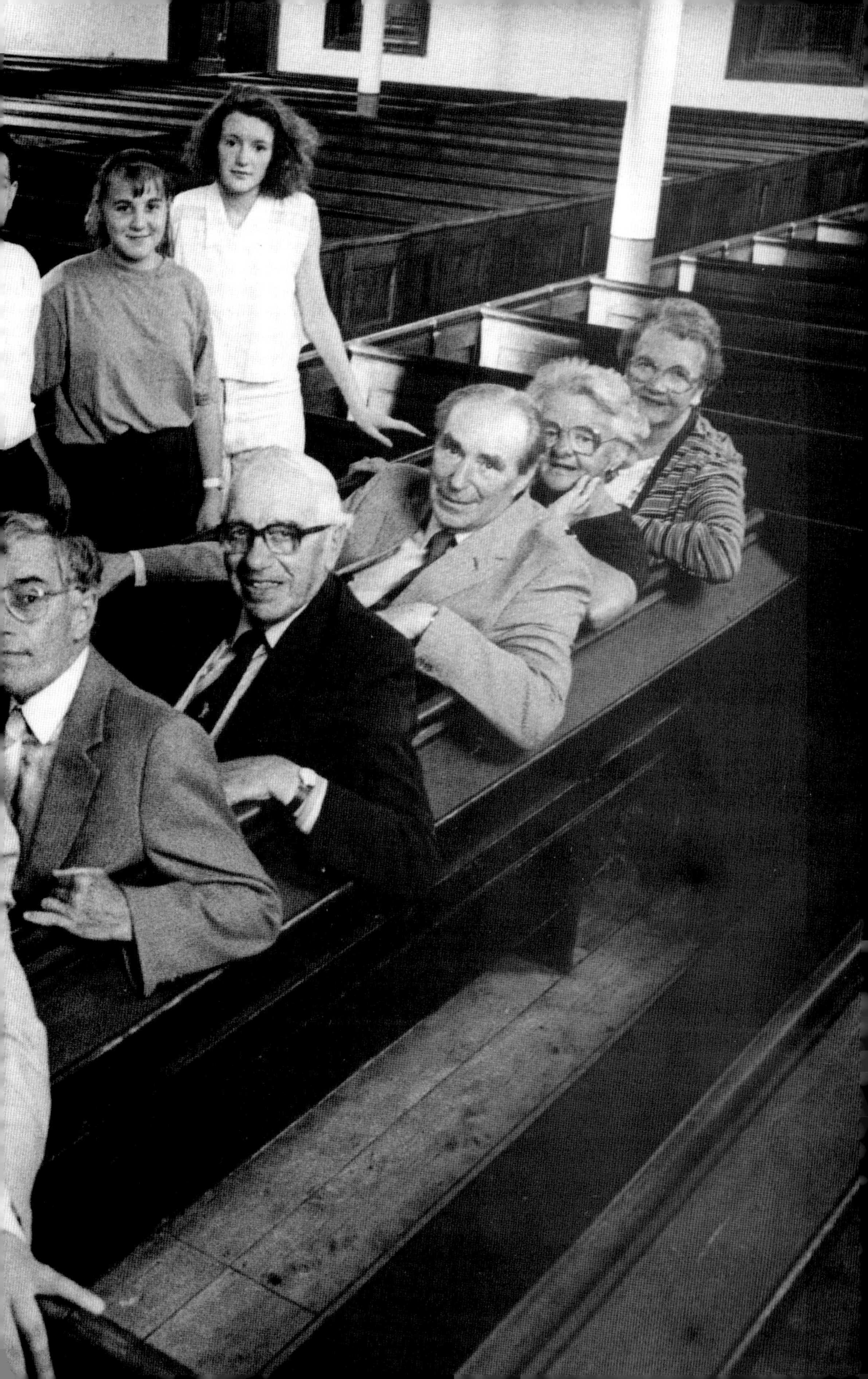

Tom and Arthur Rees pictured before a Stradey Park scoreboard telling one of its most memorable tales. Left: The complete singing Rees brothers line-up in 1948. Behind them is accompanist Ken Harries.

162

Curtain Raisers
Tom and Arthur Rees

Shortly after the Second World War an event occurred in Llanelli that was to have a significant impact on the world of entertainment in Wales. Three brothers took to the stage alongside a well-known female singer little realising that they were taking the first tentative steps on their own route to popularity.

The year was 1947, the singer was Dorothy Squires and there with her on the stage at the town's Odeon cinema were the Rees brothers — Tom, Arthur and Myrddin — with Ken Harries erstwhile organist of Cadle Chapel, Fforestfach, Swansea, who became their accompanist as a kind of 'adopted' on-stage brother.

Their performance that night went down a storm and it wasn't long before their presence was being requested all over Wales. They were signed up by Mai Jones, to sing in the much listened to and loved radio programme Welsh Rarebit and also in Workers' Playtime when it was broadcast from the Mond nickel works, in Clydach. On that occasion they appeared alongside Euryl Coslett, Cardew Robinson and Elsie and Doris Waters, known to all of course as Gert and Daisy. They also appeared for many years with Tom Pickering on Sut Hwyl? another popular radio programme involving George David, Peter Edwards, Gunstone Jones, Harriet Lewis, Ifor Rees and Dafydd Evans.

Sadly Myrddin's health failed, and Tom and Arthur were left to continue as a duo, but they were fortunate in that they remained very popular with audiences and in 1979 and 1980 they made two long playing records for Cambrian Recordings. Both were arranged and produced by Tom Hunter, while I accompanied them on piano and Clive Phillips on the organ.

Tom sang with ENSA in 1945-6 and as well as touring the United Kingdom his rich baritone voice was heard in Marseille, Malta, El Alamein, Tobruk, Cairo, Iran, Bombay, Poona, Calcutta, Rangoon, Singapore and Kuala Lumper. Other local performers in the same forces entertainment party included Megan Thomas from Llwynhendy; Meurig Price, Felinfoel; Oliver Brenton, Gorseinon; Emrys Rees, Llangennech; Hubert Francis, Gerry Evans and Joy Mexson, all from Trimsaran.

Arthur served in the Royal Navy during the war and also performed in a concert party which performed in Sydney, Australia. He was in Stars of the Services and gave a few broadcasts on 2CH Radio. On St David's Day 1945 Arthur sang with the Cymrodorion in Sydney in the presence of Australian Prime Minister Billy Hughes. Myrddin was also at sea and engaged in hazardous mine-sweeping operations for which he was awarded the British Empire Medal. No doubt there were times when he put his excellent voice to good use to raise the spirits of those around him while carrying out those tasks.

The sons of Mary and Ben Rees of Dillwyn Street, Llanelli, the three brothers also had a sister, Rachel, better known to her friends as Ray. Later in his life Tom also sang with the Belvedere Singers, a party led by well known local accompanist and soprano soloist Doris Rees.

He took part in many performances of the Messiah and his rendering of The Trumpet Shall Sound was acknowledged as being superb as were other favourite solos of his such as Brad Dynrafon, Sing a song of Sixpence and Sergeant Major on Parade. For many years he was choirmaster and also a deacon of Siloah Chapel, Llanelli.

In 1970 Arthur joined Cor Meibion Llanelli under the baton of Denver Phillips and later Eifion Thomas. As time passed he became one of its most popular soloists, appearing in this capacity for the first time in Birmingham Town Hall when his dulcet tones gave a memorable rendering of Y Fedwen Arian — the silver birch. In 1990 he was guest soloist in the choir's tour of America and Canada and, before his death some years ago, notched up more than a quarter of a century of sterling service with Cor Meibion Llanelli.

Tom died in April 1985 at the age of 75, while Myrddin passed away in September 1992 aged 77 and Arthur died eight years later in 2000. But their talents live on and like many I will always have a soft spot for the lovely music of Y Brodyr Rees — the Rees brothers.

Cruises often provided an opportunity to meet popular entertainers, such as Googie Withers, seen here with myself and her husband, actor John McCallum on board the SS Canberra.

Cruise Companion
Bruce Morrison

As well as being privileged to meet some of our greatest musical entertainers on home territory I have often encountered some very talented personalities in much different circumstances — not least while on holiday.

These distant meetings, often far away from Llanelli, brought many pleasurable moments and linked me with people I had often admired after either listening to them on the radio or watching them on TV. Some of these occasions I have already described, but there are also other remarkable people I have met while on my travels whose very presence has earned them a place in my memory. They have included people like Bruce Morrison and Googie Withers, encountered while relaxing on a cruising holiday aboard the SS Canberra and these unexpected meetings have inevitably brought precious moments and a host of happy recollections. It never failed to surprise me just how many of these had not only heard of Llanelli, but also knew where it was, had performed there and perhaps most importantly taken away with them fond recollections of their visits — a tribute the town can be proud of.

Among them was that most sincere of Scottish entertainers Bruce Morrison who captivated myself and the rest of the on-board audience with his superb talent as a singer, dancer and actor, in a production of The Good Old Days on my second night on the Canberra. It was the first of many excellent performances from him that I was to enjoy so much on the cruise. On that occasion Bruce — then just 32 — was one of nine full-time professionals, together with seven entertainment officers, who combined to form the Stadium Theatre Company, performing 30 different shows in just six weeks.

He was one of the Canberra's star entertainers and I was lucky enough to be in his company on many occasions during the voyage. During our conversations, I once asked him how he could pronounce Llanelli so well. His answer surprised me: "I was six months in repertory at the Grand Theatre, Swansea, back in 1982 under the direction of John Chilvers." One of his co-stars at that time was Menna Trussler.

One of Bruce's greatest friends is renowned Welsh actress Rachel Thomas, and to my thinking his kindness and sincerity shines through in the fact that he made a special journey from London to the Grand Theatre to see her perform in Arsenic and Old Lace some years ago. Bruce has performed at locations around the world and appeared on stage and in films with a host of stars including Alan Bates, Dora Bryan, Fiona Fullerton and Noele Gordon, Derek Nimmo and Leslie Grantham. He admitted to me that one of the highlights of his career was to perform with probably that greatest-ever British actor, Sir Laurence Olivier. His performances on Canberra in roles both straight, comic and seriously musical were all superb and the trip gave him ample opportunity to demonstrate the strength of his skills in singing, acting and dancing.

Bruce is not just a superb entertainer, he is also a lovely person to know and his company was exceedingly enjoyable. He often acted as tour escort for Canberra, and was loved by everyone for his kindness and humility. He would always wave to people on board, help the elderly and in general mix with the passengers and ultimately he became one of that voyage's most popular personalities.

I would often play piano for the passengers to have a sing-song and Bruce, after rehearsing all day, would sometimes come along and join in the fun. As he put it: "Out of respect to you Gethin — a fine pianist and entertainer." We had many good times together on board. I remember him telling me on one occasion: "I love Welsh people — nobody can narrate stories like them, and Gethin you are one of the finest Welshmen I've heard telling a story. I've laughed more on this cruise than I've done for years thanks to you."

What Bruce loved to hear were simple stories about ordinary Llanelli characters — what fun it seems people can derive from simple, down-to-earth, home-made humour. Little did he know that he helped make that cruising experience just as unforgettable for me too — and I am sure my fellow passengers would share that sentiment.

Bruce has stayed at my home on many occasions and even taken part in a Communion Service in Triniti Chapel at the request of the Minister, Rev. Russell Morgan. On one occasion he even made a special trip to Llanelli to give a free two hour concert in Triniti chapel for its organ fund. What a terrific person.

There have been occasions too when I have met up with some interesting personalities. Not least during a number of more than pleasurable stays at my favourite Scottish hotel the Banchory Lodge Hotel, Royal Deeside, run by Margaret Jaffrey a Yorkshire girl who married a Scot. I have been there quite a few times and Margaret is always the supreme host — every visit is a treat. It is like a real home from home and it has brought me some unforgettable experiences and occasional meetings with the kind of personality one would not expect. At the Ridgemount Hotel in Gower Street, London, Gwen and Roydon Rees are another couple who ensure that their Welsh guests are royally cared for while The Metropole in Llandrindod Wells is another establishment where the level of comfort and care of guests has ensured I have been more than ably looked after.

As his kilt shows, Bruce Morrison is as proud of his Scottish heritage as I am of my Welsh roots.

The 25th anniversary of Llanelli Young Music Lovers' Association in September 1995 was marked by a special event at Greenfield Chapel. Either side of me for this commemorative photograph are John Morgan, Margaret Morris-Bowen, Daphne Edwards and Teifryn Rees.

Jenny Ty Capel with some of the members of her popular and entertaining Highland Band during one of their performances..

Larger Than Life
The Jenkins Family

In the early years of the last century families were often very much larger than those we are used to today, often with 10 or maybe even more children in evidence. There were a number of these families in Llanelli who stood out for one reason or another, not least their musical prowess. It is perhaps an indication that life then was so very different.

Among one of the town's most colourful and certainly the most well known Tyisha groups was the Jenkins family of Llwyn Onn, Tyisha Road. Ann and John Jenkins were married in Triniti Chapel, in 1879 and in all they had 11 children though one of them died in infancy. They were, Mary Esther, Sam, William John, Sal, Tom, Martha Ann, Llew, Evelyn, Ben and Gwen, some of whom certainly made their mark.

Mary Esther Jenkins, the eldest, had a glorious contralto voice and became one of Wales's most famous soloists and made her name recognised on a wider stage with London and provincial concerts. She sang at the Royal Albert Hall and many other big venues with soloists such as Isobel Baillie, Elsie Suddaby, Heddle Nash, Frank Titterto, and Olive Groves. She sung under the conductorship of Sir Henry Wood, Sir Adrian Boult and Sir Thomas Beecham. She had been a pupil of Madam Clara Novello-Davies — Ivor Novello's mother — and sung with her Royal Ladies Choir.

Sam was the eldest of the boys. He possessed a glorious tenor voice, and was saluted as the Welsh Sankey, singing with Welsh evangelist Evan Roberts in the Revival of 1904-1905. Sam Jenkins too, sang all over Wales, and accompanied Evan Roberts on a long revival tour of America. In 1952 he sung Yr Hen Rebel in an open air service, outside Moriah Chapel, Loughor, when a monument to Evan Roberts was unveiled. Just a year later he died suddenly while attending the Royal National Eisteddfod in Rhyl.

Sarah Jenkins — Sal — was probably the most colourful of all the children. She was a very talented and able person. She was quick-witted, jovial in one way, and very serious and spirited in another. My uncle – Alderman John Griffiths — once described her as one of the greatest personalities he had ever known. Auntie Sal as she was called by many, could lead so beautifully in public prayer. She could address a ladies missionary meeting, and would love to take part in humourous debates or comedy situations. Once Sal Jenkins was taking part in a debate in Triniti vestry on the merits of water over milk. Sal was chosen to speak for water. She was praising it and how it readily quenched thirst, when suddenly the opposing speaker asked her what she was given to drink in a bottle as a baby. Quick as a flash she replied: "Milk and water."

The talented Jenkins family: Mary Esther, above; Sam — often referred to as the Welsh Sankey — left; and below, from left to right: Evelyn; Gwen, the youngest of the family, and Sal.

I will always remember Sal Jenkins singing a comedy item with Jenny Ty Capel and Vera Lewis in the Sunday School Christmas Tea Party — My Pretty Little Hen. She used to visit our family and we would all benefit from her exuberant personality. She taught me a little verse as a child that I will always remember and many will surely recall. It was accompanied by a series of hand actions:

> *This is the church*
> *And this is the steeple*
> *Open the door*
> *And you see the people.*

Tom Jenkins became a minister and I recall him preaching in Triniti Chapel, while Llew became a headmaster, and conducted gymanfa ganu. He was an excellent musician and a very good organist. Both he and his wife Olwen were popular adjudicators — Llew on the music side and his wife Olwen for elocution examinations. Their son Emyr Jenkins was for years the organiser of the Royal National Eisteddfod of Wales, but now holds a high post with the Welsh Arts Council in Cardiff. One of his daughters, Ffion, married William Hague former leader of the Conservative Party and another daughter, Manon, who is secretary to the Prince of Wales, married Jeremy Huw Williams, a well-known baritone.

Evelyn was the only one of the girls to marry. She married David Ebenezer from Cwmaman, Aberdare, and they lived in the family home Llwyn Onn in Tyisha Road. David Ebenezer became an elder at Triniti Chapel and for 34 years he was the general secretary of the chapel. Evelyn was a lovely character. Like the other members of the Jenkins family she was musical and possessed quite a sweet voice. Mrs Ebenezer died in 1976 at the age of 82 and a year previously she recorded with me on the organ the song that her brother Sam sang during the Revival: Yr Hen Rebel.

The youngest of the family was Gwen, one of my mother's life-long friends. Gwen lived in London until she died in 1988 and had held a high post with the Admiralty. Every Christmas and Easter Gwen would come to stay with her sister Evelyn in Tyisha Road, and it was a big night for us in Hick Street when Auntie Gwen came to supper. She and my mother, so I was told, sang a duet — Come in Little Lambs — in Triniti Chapel when they were just six years old. I am sure I won't be the only one to have clear recall of at least some of the members of the amazingly talented Jenkins family.

Nansi Richards-Jones — Telynores Maldwyn — plays the harp in traditional Welsh costume on April, 9, 1970. She was a harpist of enormous renown and even appeared on the big screen in the film, The Last Days of Dolwyn.

Heavenly Harpist
Nansi Richards-Jones

Perhaps it was no surprise that when the outstanding Welsh harp party — Cor Teyln Eryri — came to the YMCA's Brodie Hall, Llanelli for a Noson Lawen in 1944 I should be in the audience with my mother. There would have been no way that she would have allowed me to miss the experience that it undoubtedly was.

I was quite young then and recall being introduced to Nansi Richards-Jones — Telynores Maldwyn — who had been the principal harpist with Edith Evans — Telynores Eryri — assisting. The meeting had occurred at the end of the proceedings and was instigated by Olwen Williams, former head of Ysgol Dewi Sant and a deacon at Capel Als. Nansi was then 55 and Edith 49.

Thirty years elapsed before I next met them, when they gave a two-hour performance at Zion Vestry for the Llanelli Young Music Lovers' Association. Remarkably Nansi was by then 85 and Edith 79, but what a performance these two outstanding artists gave. On that evening, Nansi played many pieces on the harp including some on the complicated and difficult Triple Harp while Edith sang Cerdd Dant. Three years later Nansi, by then 88, appeared again in Llanelli and fascinated her audience at Lloyd Street Vestry with an hour-long performance. The following morning she also gave a half-hour recital at Ysgol y Strade .

Nansi Richards was born at Penybont Fawr Farm near Oswestry. She never forgot her roots, was a farm girl until she died and always said with pride: "I'm very working class." Nansi learned to play the piano at the age of eight, and the harp — then regarded as a pub instrument — at 12, much to the disgust of her grandparents. But she became one of the world's greatest harpists. At one time she was only one of three people in the world who could play the Triple Harp. It has three rows of strings and no pedals. To play the second row the harpist has to go through the two outer arrangements of strings to get into the inner ones, a difficult task, but Nansi could do it with ease.
She had been given lessons by Hungarian gypsies and especially by a Romany family — the Woods — who camped at Penybont Fawr. They were superb musicians. Five of them could play the harp and violin, and the old gent Llewellyn Wood was a wonderful triple harp player, and taught her to play.

In 1912, Nansi made a great impact on the audience and a name for herself when she took over from Bessie Jones Telynores Gwalia at the Wrexham National Eisteddfod. After that she was given the title Telynores Maldwyn — The harpist of Maldwyn — by

Among achievements that I cherish are becoming a member of the eisteddfod Bardic order, in the robes of which I am pictured here with two colleagues — Ray Thomas, of Llwynhendy and Welsh novelist Hazel Charles Evans. Inset: Some assistance in getting the look just right is always invaluable. On this occasion it was rendered by Danish friend Odile Scharbau.

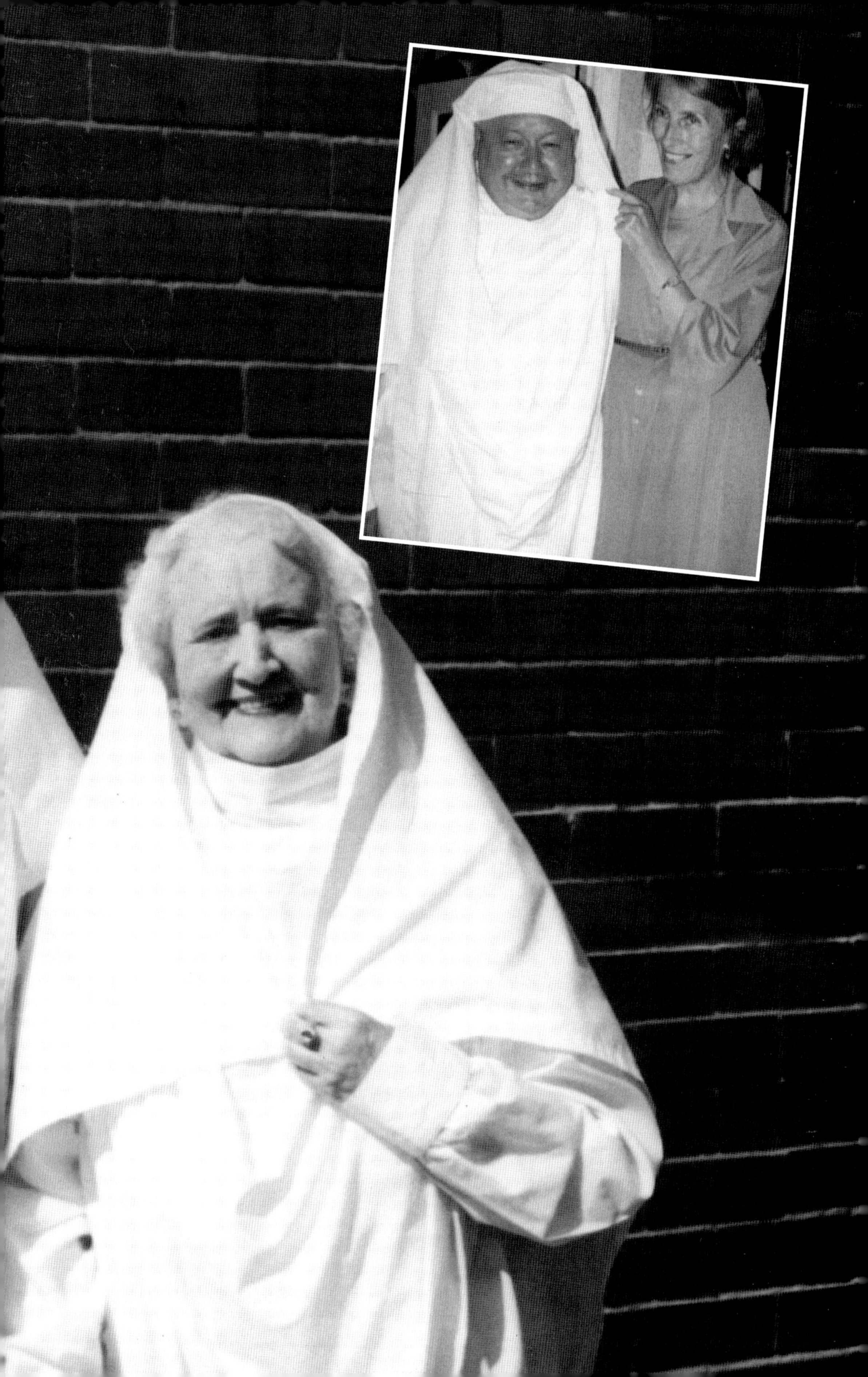

former Archdruids Eifionydd and Cadfan a title which remained with her. In her time Nansi was regarded by all as the greatest Welsh harpist in the world. She lived in London for some time and often visited 10 Downing Street to play for the Prime Minister, Lloyd George, and his family. She also played in music hall for Moss and Stoll in their theatres all around the United Kingdom.

While on a year's tour of America between 1924-1925, she had a meal with Mr Kellog and his brother Dr. Kellog and gave a harp recital at the Kellog's cornflakes factory. Nansi and the Kellog family had become great friends as a result of an incident in one hotel that she had stayed at. For breakfast the hotel waiter asked: "Would you like some Kellog's, madam?" Nansi misunderstood and replied: "No, thank you, I don't want ceiliog for breakfast, I'll have that for lunch!" She thought she was being asked if she wanted chicken which is ceiliog in Welsh. It was, apparently, after this that the cockerel began appearing on boxes of the popular breakfast cereal.

Nansi Richards even appeared on the big screen in the film, The Last Days of Dolwyn, with Emlyn Williams, Dame Edith Evans, Prysor Williams, Hugh Griffiths, and Bob Roberts the old Welsh ballad singer. During the investiture of the Prince of Wales — later Duke of Windsor — at Caernarvon Castle in 1911, Nansi played the harp and was asked by Queen Mary to give a private recital at Machynllech Mansion that evening. Within half-an-hour of her arrival at the mansion, a programme was given to her with the Royal Court of Arms on it enabling Nansi to call herself the Royal Welsh Harpist. What an honour! The Princess Royal and the Prince asked Nansi to play Gwenith Gwyn once again as it was Queen Mary's favourite. Afterwards she was summoned before Queen Mary to be thanked.

Many years later the Queen decided to honour Nansi Richards-Jones with an MBE. Nansi would not dress in anything but a plain skirt and woollen jumper to go to the palace. She was warned not to speak to the Queen, unless Her Majesty spoke to her first. But Nansi forgot everything when she saw the splendour of Buckingham Palace. Dora Herbert Jones, the famous Welsh folk singer, was also being honoured on the same day, and standing just behind Nansi. Nansi wasted no time in speaking to the Queen: "Good morning your Majesty, it's good to be here. You have a lovely little son, I hope he'll marry a Welsh girl. I met your husband in Caernarvon seven years ago — he's such a lovely man." The Queen was overwhelmed and clasped Nansi's two hands and kept her talking for a quarter-of-an-hour — proof of her respect for a great Welsh lady.

It was a privilege to know such a character as Nansi Richards-Jones, a woman who was honoured at the age of 88 at Aberystwyth University by the Prince of Wales with the Degree of Doctor of Music. This was well deserved by someone who gave 70 years or more of musical service to Wales.

Shopping Spree
Open all hours

Small, family run shops on the corner or down the street figured large in most communities in days gone by and that is certainly true of the area in which I was born into and am still proud to call home. They ministered to our every need and shopping was an experience altogether much different to the weekly trip to the supermarket that most people endure today.

New Dock Road perhaps demonstrates just how big an influence they had on our lives down the decades when brown paper bags ruled and there were no supermarkets — nor their metal basketwork trolleys. The area was once described as 'Little Llanelli beyond the station gates.' The reason is quite simply that it was almost like a complete village."

There were many business people and characters living in New Dock Road, an almost endless list of different families and diverse trades. The list here may be long but it more than proves the point that they served us with almost everything we could ever want.

There was Mrs Williams, Stanley Stores at the very top of the road selling grocery and hardware, then there was Poolman, newsagents; Daniel Jenkins, butcher; David Harris, butcher; David Williams, butcher; Hoffman, jeweller; Cohen and Berman, the Jewish drapers; Tommy Lloyd, barber; Tom Williams, cobbler; Willie Williams, herbalist; Glyn Charles, chemist; TB Gale, tobacconists; Perego's ice-cream and confectionery; WJ Thomas, butcher; Mrs Jennings, fish and chips; Charlie Brown and later Reggie Brown, fruiterers; Parkinson, greengrocer; Owen G Evans, butcher; George Thomas, ironmonger; WJ Morgan, the cinema shop; Stitson, hairdresser and Herbert Leyshon, outfitter. And all those were contained within a small area — most within the confines of just one street. What a rich shopping experience.

And if immersing oneself in it was stamina sapping then there was Jenkins' Cafe run by David and Elizabeth Jenkins and their daughter Winnie, to visit, somewhere along the way. That is one business that both survives and thrives as the Jenkins Bakery chain. In a similar vein many will have turned to fish and chip shops for their sustenance.

There were two suppliers of this traditional form of favourite food that for many at the time stood out among the others — Thomas the Chips which fried its wares in New Dock Road for over 70 years and Jenning's which was reputed to be so popular that people came from Pwll, Felinfoel and Bynea to sample the offerings of Susie and Gareth John who ran the business in later years.

Closer to my Hick Street home Jack Jones kept a grocery shop at No. 3. It was called Watson Stores after his first wife's maiden name. Idwal Williams from Stafford Street married Edna Davies of 11 Hick Street. They had a horse and cart from which they sold fish. In later years the couple ran a flourishing grocery and fruiterers in Delabeche Street. There was also John Anthony who ran a fruiterers in Tyisha Road bringing us fresh fruit and veg every Friday. He became a close friend of the family and lived in Ty'r Fran Avenue until he died.

Part of New Dock Road as it is today, complete with the original Jenkins bakery and other shops like the one on the left, all serving the community.

There was perhaps one character who stood out among all of these shop folk and traders — Annie Roberts who became known as the queen of them all. Annie lived in New Dock Street, in one of the oldest shops in Llanelli. She and her brother, Harry ran a business that had been run by her father Richard Roberts and established by his father Thomas Roberts, in the early 1800s. The shop was located opposite the town's Great Western Dock and provided provisions for the steamers that berthed there and their crews.

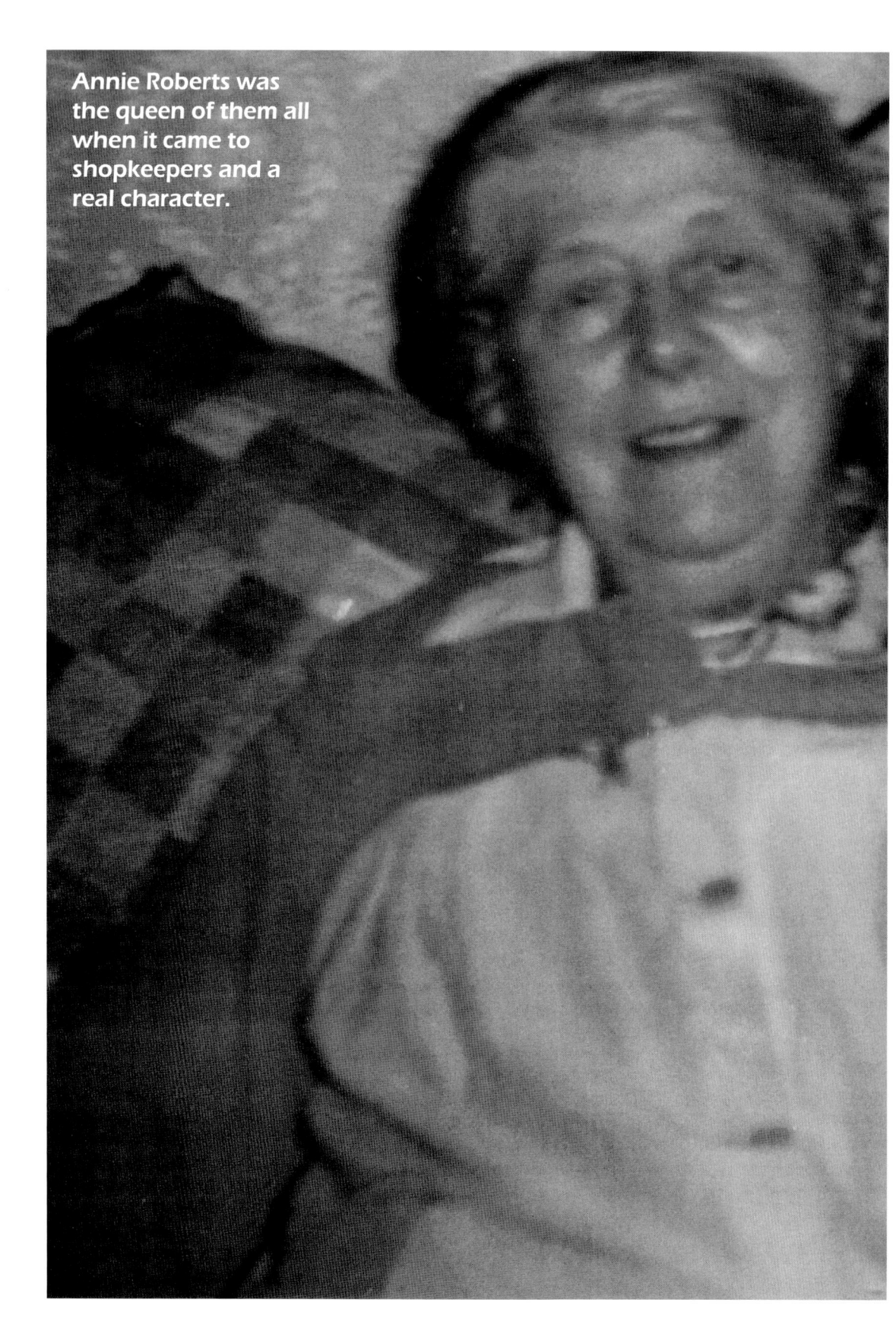

Annie Roberts was the queen of them all when it came to shopkeepers and a real character.

It was Thomas Roberts and a group of friends who started the cause of Triniti Presbyterian Chapel in the shop's warehouse in 1854 and four years later in 1858 a chapel was built in New Dock Road. There is a plaque inside today commemorating the fact.

Annie meanwhile was larger than life. She never cut or permed her hair, but always plaited it like telephone headphones. In most ways she was very old-fashioned, indeed the shop and the house was still lit by gas until 1973 when I recall electricity being installed. An intelligent and educated woman she was an avid reader and a beautiful contralto soloist, often singing in concerts in the area and in her Presbyterian Chapel. She loved opera and often recalled her visits to the Empire Theatre, Swansea to see Edith Coats in Carmen or Joan Hammond in Tosca. In later years Annie transferred her religious allegiance to Triniti, the chapel her grandfather had helped found.

Being in her company was a tonic and to hear her relate some of her stories was, at the very least entertaining. One I remember took place on a warm June evening. This was how she told me the tale: "On Monday evening I decided to go to the prayer meeting in Triniti Chapel. As I entered the vestry Mrs Tydfil Morgan was playing the piano very nicely and then everybody stood up to sing a hymn. Later, Lizzie Stewart started to pray. Seated in front of me was Miss Catherine Hughes of Trinity Road who was wearing a small fox fur. She took it off, and put it on the back of the bench.

"While Mrs Stewart was praying I heard faint, but definite, footsteps. I turned round, and to my horror saw it was Black Bob, my faithful Labrador, who had followed me to chapel. He pulled down Miss Hughes's fur and laid on it. I didn't know what to do. I pulled and tugged but could not budge the fur from under Bob. I whispered to him that he was a naughty boy, and with all my strength gave one final pull. Luckily I released the fur, just as Lizzie Stewart was ending her prayer. I quickly brushed it down with my hand and replaced it on the bench. We all sang the final hymn, and then Miss Hughes, turned around, put the fur back around her neck and commented to me on what a lovely night it was!"

People like Annie Roberts were all a part of the area's rich tapestry of life and often their premises became meeting places for friends and neighbours which in a way played a further important part in keeping the community and its spirit alive and kicking.

The back yard of our home in Hick Street was where this picture of myself and my maternal grandmother, Elizabeth Davies, with whom we then lived was taken many years ago.

Caring Community
A neighbourhood watch

Above all else in life, one thing is certain and that is that no matter where we travel and whoever we meet along the way, more often than not our journeys bring us back home — to our town, our street and to the friends and neighbours we have come to know, love and respect.

For me this is particularly true. I was born in the back bedroom of Deganwy, Hick Street, grew up there, have experienced many of life's trials and tribulations there and can even call it my home to this day. Two of my neighbours — Marion Rees and Ivy Thomas can also match this achievement. When my parents married in 1932 they moved into Deganwy to live with my grandmother on my mother's side — Elizabeth and her husband William John Davies. I remember my maternal grandparents well and growing up in Hick Street is something that produced a never-ending font of memories.

We shared the house with my mother's brother — my Uncle Davie. It was always quite a lively household and I look back fondly on those distant times. The house was a meeting point on a Saturday night for my great-grandfather on my mother's side, her two uncles, their wives and my great grandfather's brother. We were about 10 or 11 all having a meal. So the two sides of the family were represented.

My grandmother was a very generous woman and my mother followed in her footsteps. My grandmother would always make

My mother Blodwen as many Hick Street residents will remember her.

sure we had a far bigger turkey than we needed at Christmas so she could send four plates out on Christmas morning to at least a few of those less fortunate than ourselves. I never knew my paternal grandmother who was a very quiet, shy lady. But my grandfather was a character. By day he was a sample passer in the steelworks and after those stamina-sapping labours he was the choirmaster in Triniti Chapel for 10 years. He was a wonderful orator with equally wonderful handwriting even though he had left school when he was just eight years old. He taught me Worthy Is The Lamb from Handel's Messiah when I was just three.

He always said to my Auntie Gan: "This child is going to be a big musician one day look at his fingers." I was also playing on the organ even at three. As the year's passed it seemed his far off prophecy was right. I also spent a lot of time with my auntie Liz, auntie Gan and auntie Gertie — in my younger days. They were happy times, with never a dull moment. In their own, very different ways I think they all liked to spoil me. I rarely complained. Outside the confines of my family the constant of having good friends and neighbours has always been important to me and I have been fortunate to be surrounded by them in Hick Street. The families populating it have through their kindnesses and companionship always made it a pleasant haven to return to.

There are people too in the broader community who in a multitude of different ways are just as important, though often go unnoticed. These are the kind of people who sometimes we forget are there until we need them. Our emergency services are a broad example — always there in the background, ready to rally to our assistance.

In a way this is the kind of community category under which I would place the important service rendered by the medical staff in whose trust we place our health. In my case that has meant long family links with Fairfield surgery, its doctors, nurses and receptionists. The principals in the practice have, down the years included doctors JAA Hunter; Graham Hodges, Norman Harris and latterly Dr. Alan Howarth. To these and also Peter Cnudde, the young Belgian surgeon who early in 2006 operated on my hip at the Prince Phillip Hospital, Llanelli, and all of the caring nursing staff of Ward 8 who attended to me, I owe a great debt.

Additionally Norma and Eira are two of Fairfield surgery's receptionists from recent years who were real characters — everyone loved them and they helped make sure things ran smoothly. Some may remember before them the irrepressible Miss Margrave. She was the dispenser, belonged to the old school and ran everything with a firm hand. Most would admit to being just a little afraid of her.

I salute too the work of the many carers who dependably and uncomplainingly go about their duties throughout our communities. I can offer first hand confirmation that their services and attention makes life more bearable. For me they are epitomised by my

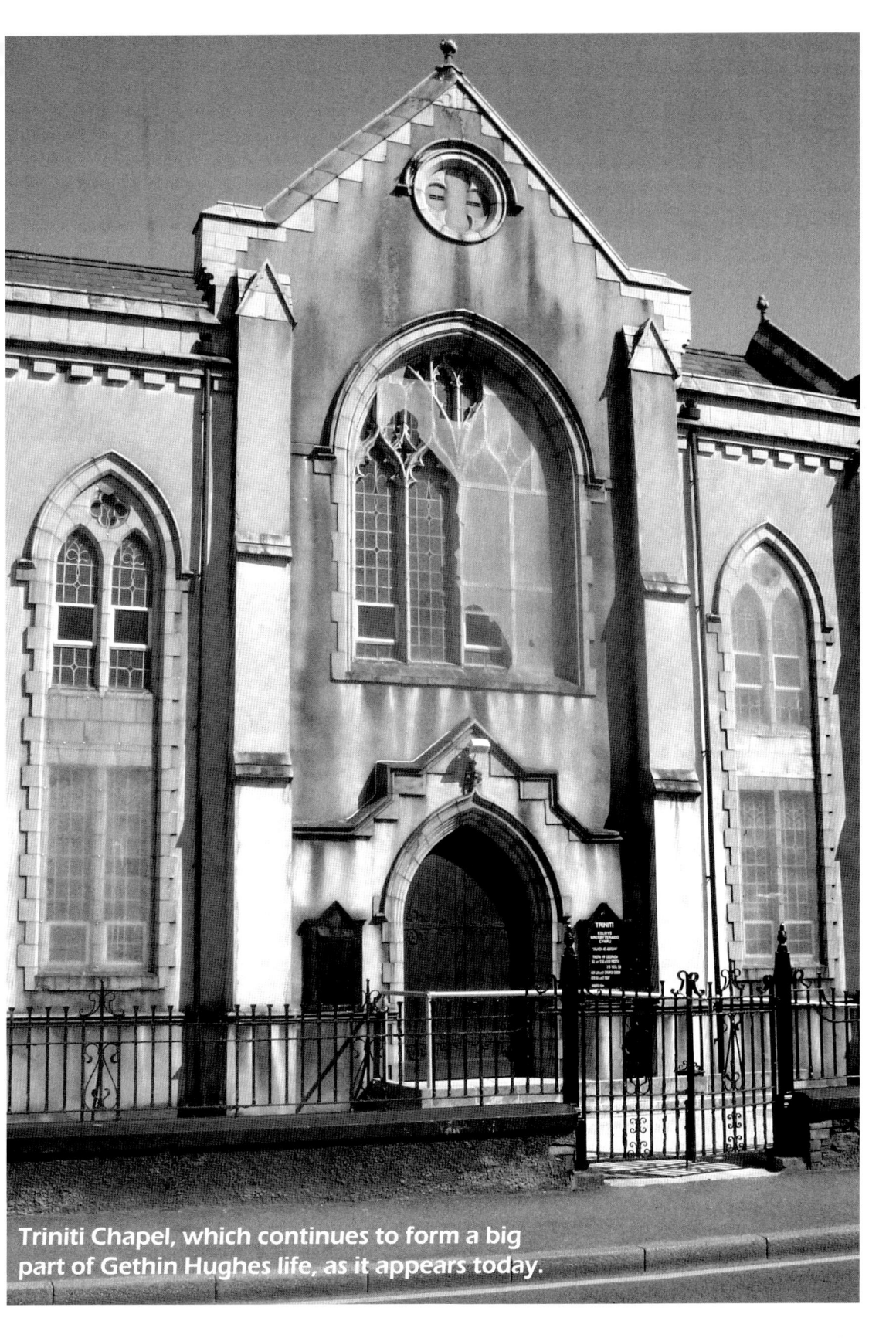

Triniti Chapel, which continues to form a big part of Gethin Hughes life, as it appears today.

carers — Sandra Taylor with help of her husband Terry who are also the Trinti Chapel caretakers; Theresa White with her two children Chad and Ashby; also the present minister of Triniti Rev. Eifion Roberts and his wife Alwen. To me they are all a great help. To the wider world they are truly representative of many others who give of their time and energy to embrace the feeling of community spirit.

Add to that the privilege of sharing so many of my experiences with long standing, close friends in and around Llanelli and life has fortunately brought me many more ups than downs. Without all of these caring friends and neighbours and through them, a multitude of pleasant memories, my life would indeed have been a far poorer experience.

In their way all these community stalwarts are superstars too, just like many of those I have encountered throughout my life and recalled in this book, personalities who have made my musical world such a tuneful place in which to exist. To them all I say thank you and I hope that in their company I have indeed always been natural!

Never be sharp,
Never be flat,
ALWAYS be natural.
— Roy Castle